Power Market Risk:
How To Survive (& Prosper)
In Crazy Times

Thinking *Energy*
An imprint of The *Thinking* Companies Inc.
Falmouth, ME.
www.thinkingenergy.com

POWER MARKET RISK

HOW TO SURVIVE (& PROSPER) IN CRAZY TIMES

Shirley S. Savage & Peter R. Savage

POWER MARKET RISK:
HOW TO SURVIVE (& PROSPER) IN CRAZY TIMES

Thinking Energy
An imprint of The Thinking Companies, Inc.
PMB 353, US Route One
Falmouth ME 04105

Copyright © 2003 by Shirley S. Savage and Peter R. Savage

Text Layout by *Thinking Artists*
Cover Design by LSW Graphics, Falmouth, ME

All rights reserved. No part of this book may be reproduced in whole or part without written permission from the publisher, except by reviewers who may quote brief excerpts in connection with a review in a newspaper, magazine or electronic publication; nor may any part of this book be reproduced, stored in a retrieval system, or be transmitted in any form or by any means, including electronic, mechanical, photocopying, recording, or other, without written permission from the publisher. A similar restrictive license shall be applied to buyers of any versions of the book sold electronically in PDF format.

Although the authors and publisher have made every effort to ensure the accuracy and completeness of information contained in this book, we assume no responsibility for errors, inaccuracies, omissions or any minor inconsistencies. The book does not intend to offer legal or accounting advice, and readers should use their own common sense or consult with a legal or accounting professional for specific applications.

This book is an complete revision and major expansion of *"Power Market Risk Management: A Survival Guide"*, published by Financial Times Energy in 2000. Copyright was reassigned by the beneficial owner, The McGraw-Hill Companies, to The Thinking Companies in 2002, under the terms of the original 1999 author's contract with FT Energy.

ISBN: 0-9727037-0-5

Printed/ bound in the USA by Grapheteria, Inc., Portland, ME

**Attention Corporations, Universities, Colleges
and Professional Organizations**:
Quantity discounts are available on bulk purchases of this book for educational or gift purposes or as loyalty benefits to clients. Electronic versions are available on request. Please contact: Marketing Dept., The Thinking Companies, Inc., PMB 353, US Route One, Falmouth ME 04105. Phone: (207)-829-3223. Fax: (207)-829-2722. E-Mail: riskbook@thinkingenergy.com

POWER MARKET RISK:
HOW TO SURVIVE (& PROSPER) IN CRAZY TIMES

by
Shirley S. Savage & Peter R. Savage

Table Of Contents

	Preface	**9**
1	Why You Need Risk Management More Than Ever	**13**
2	Setting It Up: It's All About Governance	**19**
3	On The Firing Line: The Chief Risk Officer	**30**
4	A Quick Look At Futures, Derivatives & Indices	**41**
5	Market Risk Essentials	**49**
6	What You Need To Know About The Trading Culture	**59**
7	How Well Do You Know This Guy, Really? : Human Resource Issues	**71**
8	Credit Risk: What You Don't Know *Can* Hurt You	**83**
9	The Fine Print: Legal & Accounting Issues	**99**

Continued >

Contents (*continued*)

10 Knowledge, Not Data: **123**
   Using CI To Avoid Pitfalls

11 Uneven Playing Fields: **133**
   Dealing With Rigged Markets

12 The Apple Of Temptation: **163**
   Run An Honest Business

13 How Risk Management Can **171**
   Save The Day

14 Stemming The Tide Of **181**
   Stakeholder Discontent

15 Rolling The Crystal Ball: **191**
   Some Predictions

Resources & Reading **197**

Preface

When we embarked on this project, we imagined we would merely be providing a timely revision, a second edition of our earlier best-selling *"Power Market Risk Management: A Survival Guide"*. The idea was to show how the lessons of risk management could have been better applied in the recent California power crisis, the collapse of Enron, and other market upheavals. The message was to have been, subtly stated: *"If only you'd listened..."*

But it's not that simple. What we've discovered during our research is even more shocking than people "not listening." It's that, throughout the power industry, there's still a fundamental lack of understanding of what Risk Management is about. Its purpose, and even its day-to-day practice, remains unclear to many. Billions of dollars are at risk, simply because many companies have failed to grasp the basic point: that RM is not about making money, but how to insure against losing it.

Risk management will always tend to clip the peaks of success, but it will *always* minimize the penalties of failure. It's like insurance, it's like thrift, it's like carefully chosen investments; in the long term you reap rewards.

This book isn't focused on how to handles futures, derivatives and other market instruments, although we'll explain the fundamentals. Instead, it's intended to be an education in real world dynamics for board members, senior executives and others who have a murky idea of how risk management works.

In this book, we'll tell you about current best practices; give you some advice on how to make RM work for you; how to measure its success; and how to avoid pitfalls. We discuss improvements that companies are making in the post-crisis era.

What we can't tell you is how to behave ethically! The lessons of the California crisis are many, but greed and stupidity played an important role in events there in 2000-2001. Deregulation of utilities provided the catalyst. The fall of Enron, like that of many US businesses lately, was largely the result of management dishonesty, hubris and greed. And a simple lack of common sense.

If we accomplish our aim – if you take away one useful lesson from this book (though there are simply hundreds) – let it be: 'If it looks too good to be true, then it probably is.'

The book didn't emerge from thin air. We are grateful to the many people in the power markets who graciously gave their time, guidance, and advice to us on this second edition as well as the first edition of the book.

Special thanks to Andrea S. Kramer of McDermott, Will & Emery for allowing me to quote excerpts from her various risk management works and for reviewing several of the chapters; and to The Group Of Thirty for granting us permission to quote from The Holy Grail, aka *Derivatives: Practices and Principles*.

A heartfelt thank you to those who were kind enough to share their knowledge and expertise about risk management for this version of the book: Mark Williams of Boston University, Craig Goodman of The National Energy Marketers Association, Scott Smith and David M.

Hagelin of American Electric Power, G. Patrich Simpkins and Carol Peters of TXU, Felix Carabello and William Burks of the Chicago Mercantile Exchange, Valerie Bergman Cooper of the Weather Risk Management Association, and 'Anonymous.'

We would also like to thank Harry Sachinis of Platt's for granting us the rights to publish this revised edition, Lola Lea for careful reading of the manuscript and advice, Leolyn Wood for the cover design, Cosmo Di Piero at Grapheteria for helping us get the book in print, and Peter Galuszka for giving us the line we've never forgotten: "How well do you know this guy, really?" Finally, we'd like to thank G.J.U. Rinpoche for his support..

While these people gave freely of their time and advice, any omissions or inconsistencies are, of course, our own.

This book is loosely based on the earlier work, *Power Market Risk Management: A Survival Guide,* by Shirley Savage, written in 1999 and published by Financial Times Energy in 2000. It is a complete revision and expansion of that earlier work, based on changes that have occurred during the intervening period, and reflects a new consensus on how risk management should be practiced in the power and energy industries.

A notable non-contributor to either the previous work, or this book, is Enron. When we approached the company in 1999 we were told: "we're writing our own book on risk management, and we don't want to talk." Perhaps they would have better used their precious time to read ours instead, and mind the ship?

SSS & PRS
North Yarmouth, ME
November 2002

Chapter 1

Why You Need Risk Management More Than Ever

Risk is a four-letter word with powerful connotations. On the positive side, risk indicates taking a chance, one that has a beneficial outcome. After all, if someone is called a 'risk taker,' it's usually meant as a compliment. But if taking a risk turns out badly – and let's face it, that can happen – we say that person engaged in 'risky business.' If we are afraid of risk, we describe ourselves as risk averse.

Risk is the great unknown. You can ignore it. But it will be to your detriment to do so. Or you can try to understand it and manage it. Risk is not static. What constitutes the great unknown is constantly changing. What is risky today may be different than what's risky next year.

There's no clearer example of the quixotic nature of risk than the power markets. Moving from a regulated to a deregulated market has proved to be a painful learning experience. The safe, secure world of regulation has given way to a world where uncertainty

POWER MARKET RISK

reigns and where some companies have done their best to manipulate the market for their own benefit. A certain amount of disruption was expected in making the change. But the unprecedented manipulation of the energy markets by Enron and others has set off pandemonium. And it's triggered a real crisis of confidence and trust – in companies, employees, and senior management.

If you are the least bit risk averse, no doubt recent events make you want to run and hide. Please don't. You can't avoid risk. But you can manage it. And by managing risk, you can help your company protect and grow revenues.

People unfamiliar with the concept of risk management unfortunately do think it's synonymous with "risky business." The term conjures up images of unscrupulous traders racking up millions of dollars in profits in precarious dealings while management declares, "I don't know anything about derivatives, but what that trader is doing is miraculous. Good job." But when the market turns against the trader and those profits are erased in a flash, management affirms, "I always knew we couldn't trust that guy." However, these images aren't reflective of risk management because the basic fact is: risk management isn't gambling.

Simply put, risk management is a practice of identifying the risks affecting your business and finding ways to mitigate the impact of those risks. It's anticipating negative factors that could affect your revenues and finding ways to counteract the negative effects. For instance, the way to counteract market risk involves using financial instruments such as futures contracts and derivatives to protect your company from the ups and downs of the market.

Risk management is a structured discipline that uses well defined policies and procedures to minimize a company's credit, market, business or operational risks. Risk management is a way of looking at an unstable factor like fluctuating fuel prices and finding ways to offset the risk of that instability. Senior management, including the board of directors, should be directly involved in setting those policies and procedures. When implemented properly, risk management can help a company protect its revenues and also help mitigate problems with trades and with counterparty credit. By using risk management techniques, a company will know, on a daily basis, if any of its trading positions are out of balance with its agreed upon trading policies. Further, risk management practices will alert a company to changes in a counterparty's credit rating. The company can then make adjustments to mitigate the impact of a counterparty defaulting on an agreement.

Risk management isn't something that a company does one year and not the next; rather, it's a long-term strategy. While benefits of a risk management program may be apparent in the first few years, to be really effective, it must be in place over time. That's not to say that the program won't change as business changes. It will. But a company must make a long-term commitment to a risk management program and see that it is established as part of the fabric of the company.

Okay, that's all well and good in theory, you might be thinking. But what about in practice? What about all the energy companies that have seen troubled times because of rogue traders, shifty CEOs and CFOs, and aggressive trading? Weren't these companies supposed to be experts in risk management?

Sure, these companies were held up to be examples of risk management experts. But in reality, their risk management programs were lacking in breadth and oversight. A solid risk management program covers the entire company, not just the trading group.

That's just the point made by G. Patrich Simpkins, executive vice president and chief risk officer (CRO) of TXU. "When things like Enron happen, people say, 'Where was the risk manager?' The truth is, if one digs deep into a company, many times risk managers are handling risk practice or risk control," says Simpkins. "That manager wasn't looking at telecomm, or generation, or the retail operation, or the water division that the company just happens to own. He was just looking at trading. Well, why is that? In the energy business, it's this way because trading is relatively new and participants are a little tentative. Risk falls within four broad categories – market, credit, operational, and business risk. Inside of business risk, companies' have customer attrition risk issues, for example. System risk and contract risk fall within operational risk. Counterparty risk falls within credit, according to Simpkins.

"Enron probably had as good a system as anyone," notes Simpkins. "It had better personnel on average than most. So you say, 'My gosh, what happened?' The reality is that the risk focus was centered on trading, which wasn't the crux of the problem. The crux of the problem was operational risk and operational risk controls. The risk manager wasn't really the person the company was looking to 'manage risk.' The person who managed risk was the same person responsible for bringing in revenue. That's a governance issue and also an operating risk issue," Simpkins points out.

Governance has become increasingly important as companies seek to rebound from the crisis created by Enron, the California energy markets, and greedy senior management. When profits are rolling in and stock prices are rising, we might not be as attentive to how a company is being run. We just want to let the good times roll. But when we're faced with steep declines in stock prices and deficits, we start looking for someone or something to blame. Frankly, we think that's not the answer. A more constructive approach is to realize that there are huge gaps not only in governance, but also in business ethics and responsibility, and to seek ways to close those gaps and promote honest and ethical business conduct. In fact, that's what a good risk management program should promote.

"One of the key responsibilities of a risk manager or chief risk officer is to make sure that the company is honest with itself," notes Simpkins. "I can't overemphasize that enough. Sometimes when companies get caught up in transactions and prospective transactions; it's amazing what they can justify to themselves. Stakeholders trust you when you spend capital. I think it's the responsibility of the CRO to say: 'Would my average stakeholder sink his money into this transaction?' Because at the end of the day, that's exactly what's going on. But at a lot of companies, the CRO isn't given the platform from which to raise those objections."

Having a risk management shop is becoming more and more an essential part of doing business, points out Mark Williams, risk management expert in the finance and economics department at Boston University. And rating agencies are requiring companies to have strong risk management departments. Several years ago, companies that had a risk management shop were demonstrating that they were progressive. Now, Williams contends, the view is "if you do not have strong risk management capabilities and senior level manager, then that's inappropriate."

When energy companies talk to people in the investment community now, companies need to incorporate a full discussion of risk management polices and practices,

Williams notes. It's not just an internal control function any more. So there's a structural change in risk management that's being dictated by external sources including the capital marketplace, third-party rating agencies as well as equity and debt holders.

The advantages of setting up a risk management program are many. In fact, if a company doesn't have a risk management program, then it likely isn't running its business properly. A company may feel that there are more pressing needs in this increasingly competitive market, but that's short-sighted: if there are tools and strategies that can be used to bolster revenue and maintain its credit rating, a company would be wise to avail itself of those strategies and tools. "There's no such thing as a risk-free deal," notes AEP's Chief Risk Officer Scott Smith.

What's more frightening: running a business that operates with honesty and integrity or a business that relies on murky practices? Risk management gives you the tools to ensure that your company operates with integrity and enables shareholder trust. What's scary about that?

Chapter 2

Setting It Up: It's All About Governance

Risk management, like most management practices, should be part of the standard processes of any successful company. It needs to be instituted as part of the company's culture. All management is an ongoing process, and risk management is no exception. However, there are principles that guide risk management, and any company seeking to set up a risk management group would do well to understand that risk management is a discipline.

Setting up a risk management program isn't simple. There are a number of steps that must be taken if the program is to manage risk effectively for the company. It's crucial for a risk management program to have a solid structure with good reporting lines and oversight. In addition, you need to have good people running the program.

Risk management shouldn't be confined only to managing trading or market operations. Business, credit, legal and operational risks also must be considered. Business risk is anything that threatens a company from reaching its goals. These days, one of the main business risks for companies in the power markets is maintaining investment grade status with the ratings agencies. Operational risk normally refers to failures related to people, technology, and external events. Credit risk is the possibility that a counterparty will default. Legal risk is the likelihood that a contract can't be enforced. We will cover market, credit and legal risks in separate chapters. Since operational and business risks are intertwined in the day-to-day workings of companies, those risks will be addressed in the "real-life" examples of risk management throughout the book.

Ideally, a company's risk management program will oversee all of the company's operations. This is the idea behind enterprise risk management. Companies that handle risk successfully do so because the risk management program extends to all of the business areas of these companies. As we'll see later, enterprise risk management has helped companies like AEP and TXU through the recent events in the power markets.

Strong Corporate Governance

To be successful in managing risk, be it commodity or finance related, a company must have a structure and plan for developing the program, running the program, and evaluating the program. This structure must be integrated into the company because it affects everyone from the board of directors to the to the accounting department. That's a point emphasized clearly by current events.

Corporate governance has become one of the most important issues for companies in the last year. We've seen that chaos results when governance is lacking. Strong corporate governance has always been advised for companies dealing in markets since the early 1990s. In 1993, The Group of Thirty, a private nonprofit organization, explicitly called on companies to have solid corporate governance for derivatives trading programs. The United States General Accounting Office (GAO) also believes in the importance of oversight. In 1994, the GAO issued a report, *Financial Derivatives: Actions Needed to Protect the Financial System,* which pointed out the need for governance in any risk management program. In 2002, two nongovernment groups, the National Energy Marketers Association and the Committee of Chief Risk Officers, set out guidelines for governance in the energy markets. We'll look specifically at those guidelines in a later chapter. For the moment, let's take a look at the recommendations from the GAO.

The GAO states unequivocally that active oversight by senior level management and outside auditors is necessary for an effective risk management system. "Strong corporate governance, which includes competent supervision by firms' boards of directors and senior management, is needed to ensure that such systems are in place and functioning as anticipated," says the GAO.

"The audit committees of the boards of directors should provide oversight of internal and external auditor activity to ensure appropriate focus and to ensure that management is not overriding internal controls. Although accountability for controlling the risks associated with derivatives rests with the boards of directors and senior management, auditors play a primary role in testing compliance with risk management policies and controls. Management accountability for internal controls can be enhanced through annual formal assessments and public reporting on the effectiveness of risk management policies and controls. Review by the external auditor should enhance the reliability of such reports. The likely effect of such assessments and reporting would be to increase the attention given to derivatives risk management by senior management and boards of directors."

Although written several years ago, the GAO's recommendations remain solid for today's companies. How can that be, you might be saying, in light of Enron and Arthur Anderson? Because the GAO is recommending sound principles such as management accountability and public reporting. These principles were largely ignored at companies that have recently hit the skids. Corporate sleight of hand isn't the same as management accountability. When ethics and principles get thrown out the window as companies chase bigger profits, chaos results. If a company wants to run a good risk management program, then governance and controls should be paramount.

Role Of The Board Of Directors

The burden of setting up a risk management group lies with the Board of Directors. The Board is key to drawing up the principles for the risk management program and overseeing it.

Andrea S. Kramer, a partner at McDermott, Will & Emery, in her guide entitled "Items to Consider for Trading and Derivatives Policies, Guidelines, Controls and Internal Procedures," has a checklist of duties to be performed by the board of directors as they oversee a risk management program. Kramer's list of responsibilities states that the board should:
- Set out the risk management objectives for the company before risk management strategy is implemented.
- Undertake periodic board review and approval of risk management policies and procedures (particularly those that define risk tolerance).
- Know what derivatives the company uses and the at-

tendant risks.
- Annually review and approve general authorizing guidelines and procedures. Allocate sufficient resources to record, manage, and control derivatives risks.
- Be regularly informed of risk exposures and material risk management issues.
- Exercise overall supervision of operations, while leaving day-to-day operations to management.
- Provide that specified individuals or committees within management may approve exceptions to the quantitative guidelines with material exceptions reported to the board of directors.
- Ensure that the company's risk monitoring and risk management operations have the necessary authority and resources to accomplish their management control objectives.

Structuring Oversight

Setting up the proper layers of oversight is a vital part of any risk management program. One of the main components of oversight is establishing a risk management committee or an exposure management committee.

For example, at one utility, the exposure management committee handles the oversight function. This committee is formed of upper level management and approves trading strategies and limits. But there is oversight of this committee as well. The board of directors must approve the exposure management committee's trading procedures and policies.

McDermott, Will & Emery's Kramer has also developed guidelines for the risk management committee. She says that:
- The risk management functions should be independ-

ent from the management of the trading activities.
- Trading risks and profits and losses should be reported at least daily to managers who supervise, but do not themselves conduct, trading activities.
- The head of risk management activities should have sufficient authority and stature to provide an effective independent assessment of risk exposure levels.
- Traders' compensation should not be tied too closely to the profitability of trading.
- Reports should allow management to accurately evaluate risk exposures and the company's overall risk profile.
- Risk management methods should be reviewed at least annually, to evaluate the assumptions used to measure risk and limit exposures.
- There should be a formal review process in place for new products to develop appropriate policies and controls and to integrate new products into the risk management and measurement system.
- The responsibilities of the risk management committee to issue detailed implementation requirements should be clearly set out.
- Meetings of the risk management committee should be regularly scheduled.
- Reporting requirements of the risk management committee should be clearly set out.

Expertise

When a company decides to set up a risk management group and a trading group, it must look for experienced personnel. In some respects, risk management and trading are specialized skills. Certainly these skills can be learned. But, it benefits a company to hire experienced personnel, especially if a company is new to risk management.

Notes Craig Goodman, President of the National Energy Marketers Association: "For a hundred years, utilities relied on regulators as their risk managers. So it is not surprising that regulated utilities, who relied on guaranteed rates of return on virtually all of their investments, did not consider risk management as a core competency. It's not a skill set that was required by a regulated utility or that was fostered in a regulated environment. As we restructure, it is vital to remember that risk management skills must reside in the unregulated marketplace and they must outperform government-based risk management via ratepayer guarantees."

The Group of Thirty suggests that companies "ensure that their derivatives activities are undertaken by professionals in sufficient number and with the appropriate experience, skill levels, and degrees of specialization. These professionals include specialists who transact and manage the risk involved, their supervisors, and those responsible for processing, reporting, controlling, and auditing activities."

Further, attorney Andrea Kramer suggests that: "comprehensive background checks should be conducted prior to employment or involvement with trading operations." She advises that employees should be checked regarding prior and pending litigation, prior employment history, and prior and pending disciplinary matters. (For more about hiring issues, see Chapter 7).

While it is important that those doing the risk management and trading have expertise, The Group of Thirty also points out that managers who oversee these functional areas must also understand both derivatives and the broader business context of risk management.

POWER MARKET RISK

Communicating to the Top

There's little point in having skilled professionals doing the trading and risk management if the senior managers don't understand what these professionals are doing. Senior management must comprehend futures and derivatives trading, and risk management; otherwise they won't be able to provide quality oversight. Unless senior management is savvy to the markets, the risk manager and trader will have a difficult time communicating with senior management. The ability to communicate effectively is paramount to any risk management program. Imprecise communication leads to mistakes that may be costly. As a company embarks upon a risk management program, it will be useful for senior managers to have some training in risk management concepts.

Various organizations offer conferences or seminars on risk management, and often risk management consultants make themselves available for educational sessions. Being informed is not a luxury and having some knowledge of risk management will help senior management make good decisions about the company's risk strategy.

Keeping top-level management informed isn't a chore, it's a necessity, a key element in any risk management program. And it's one of the important elements of the chief risk officer's job. There are many ways to do this – daily reports or weekly reports to upper level management. The Board of Directors should receive monthly or quarterly reports, at the very least.

Here's how it works at American Electric Power (AEP): "The important thing is that you provide to senior management and the Board a risk profile of the organization," comments Scott Smith, chief risk officer at AEP. "I call it the 'USA Today' approach where all the risk limits and measures are on one page." To make it easier for users to quickly grasp the current risk management situation, Smith takes a cue from stoplights. "A red light would be any limit excess. A yellow light would be any call triggers. Before we hit the limit, we're going to have a yellow light. That means we're going to have a lot of discussion, so we don't get into the red territory. And, then obviously, we have the green light."

"The senior management team gets a weekly report on the situation," Smith says. "They can take a look at it and say here's green, here's red, and here's yellow. Someone reading the report can say: 'If it's green, well, I've got 20 other things to worry about. If it's yellow, I'm going to read it. If it's red, I'm going to give Scott a call and ask what are you doing to get back within limits?' I find it a very effective tool. You get calls from the line, asking 'Am I going to be a red or a yellow this week?'"

Despite the best efforts by a risk management group to report daily and weekly to upper level management, it's often the case that, despite good intentions, the risk reports aren't being read or commented upon. This is a potentially dangerous situation and one that may cause trouble for the company in the long term. The Government Accounting Office points out that "weak corporate governance systems are a common feature of failed financial institutions."

Authority

Once a company has risk management and trading staff in place, The Group of Thirty suggests that senior management "designate who is authorized to commit their institutions to derivatives transactions." Authority may be given to certain individuals holding specific positions within the company. Management may decide to impose limits on certain types of transactions. Who is authorized

POWER MARKET RISK

to conduct risk management activities should be known within the company.

Avoiding unauthorized trades is good advice. Further, The Group of Thirty advises, "participants should communicate information on which individuals have the authority to commit to counterparties." And "they should recognize, however, that the legal doctrine of 'apparent authority' may govern the transactions they enter into, and that there is no substitute for appropriate internal controls."

A useful skills list for employees with trading authority has been developed by attorney Kramer. She says these employees must:

- Have a working knowledge of the relevant market.
- Have a familiarity with all derivatives that may be used.
- Have a solid understanding of the company's specific exposures and hedging strategies.
- Understand the risk exposures arising from the product in question.
- Have an understanding of risk management guidelines.
- Have an understanding of the management control procedures for documenting, recording, and reporting the transaction.

For those traders "with discretionary trading authority, individual trading limits must be specified," insists Kramer. These limits would include "limits on net open positions; limits on options and leveraged derivatives transactions; and limits and trade restrictions in designated products."

Controls

Establishing a system of internal controls which protect the risk management program is essential. According to attorney Kramer, internal controls should include the following:

- Separation of functions and duties;
- Complete separation of trading, back office operations, and middle office;
- Daily reevaluation of trading positions, including illiquid and long-dated contracts, which should be independent of the trading personnel and management;
- Limited access to deal and system data;
- Independent validation process; and
- An integrated company-wide system for measuring and limiting risk.

Other controls should focus on verifying elements of the trade, including confirmations and authorizations, and establishing a third-party review to audit policy compliance.

Now that you have the structure of the risk management program set up, you need someone to run it. That's the job of the Chief Risk Officer.

Chapter 3

On The Firing Line: The Chief Risk Officer

Once your Board of Directors has laid the groundwork for the risk management group, you've got to have someone run the day-to-day operation of the group. That role falls to the chief risk officer (CRO). Just as people have a misconception about a risk management program (it isn't gambling), there's a misconception about the role of the CRO. The CRO isn't a referee or a cheerleader. He or she is responsible for overseeing the risk management program on a daily basis and seeing that the company is adhering to the policies and procedures set by the Board. It's a very active role, and a tough one.

"The good risk managers are the pessimistic types. I like to call them the 'Eeyores' of the organization," comments Mark Williams, risk management expert, finance and economics department of Boston University. "They aren't the optimistic front office saying, 'I'm going long and I'll make lots of money.' We've found that having Eeyores in organizations are quite helpful in getting a thorough flushing out of the pros and cons of different strategies. Groups function much better when there are differences in background and opinions."

POWER MARKET RISK

The CRO function is a relatively new one. It highlights an evolution in risk management from risk control to having a risk manager to having a CRO. That evolution is driven by a change in philosophy as well. Instead of focusing solely on return, power market companies are now taking at look at how risk can affect a company's return. This change was by and large spurred by the equity markets.

"The equity markets were a harbinger of change" regarding the role of the risk manager, says Williams. "Over the last decade, in the stock market, investors previously would make investment decisions based on the return of equities to alternatives asset classes e.g., bonds, rather than focusing on the associated risk." But now due to the increase in stock market volatility, investors are now realizing that there's true risks related to seeking such returns, Williams observes.

The same holds true for the power markets. In a lot of cases, there wasn't a culture of risk with utilities. Utilities focus was limited to return. And that caused problems when utilities launched trading companies and did not have the adequate systems or staffing to measure, monitor and control risk, says Williams.

In the power markets, a number of companies in the latter half of the 1990's set up power trading companies in an attempt to enhance revenue. Such companies made the fatal flaw of focusing on the returns and not the associated risk.

There have been four clear profitability phases in energy trading so far, Williams contends. In 1998, it was extremely profitable. In 1999, it was profitable. In 2000, after California, it was questionable. By late 2001 and 2002, profits were negative and having trading operations was considered toxic.

What was the turning point? "After all the egregious profits that were made in California, it became obvious that the return companies received came with clear risks," states Williams. It was a realization of a zero sum game - the profits that a few power traders made e.g., El Paso, Enron and Williams were at the expense of other power traders who were short electricity, Williams contends. "It's was the rude awakening that with higher return comes higher risk."

That realization has also altered the way that traders are viewed by the power markets. In the heyday of energy trading, the front office was trading and it drove the bus, Williams comments. Now, the pure speculative traders don't drive the bus. The middle office – risk managers -- is taking a more front and center role. Job number one for all energy companies is now risk mitigation. "The overriding objective of an energy company now is to maintain profitability, reduce quarterly earnings volatility so you aren't whacked by Wall Street, and enhance shareholder value. It's much more focused on the heart of risk management – is the level of risk taken worth the level of return," Williams comments.

The focus is now on hedging and asset optimization, not pure speculative trading. The skill set needed is more quantitative, says Williams. In asset optimization, the primary focus is on risk mitigation related to locking in a given spark spread (usually defined as options that reflect the difference in value between the cost of the energy used to produce electricity and the electricity itself). As a result, the volume of trades completed on a daily basis has decreased significantly as has overall trade volume. Quantitative models are used to create assessments, correlations, prices and forecasts, points out Williams. Then the models are used to follow market pricing trends. A few days or weeks later, you might decide to lock in a favorable hedge position. The hedge is then monitored to on-going market prices and conditions to see if it's efficient and if the targeted profit margins being maintained. Really, it's monitoring the spark spread, Williams points out. You have to understand the risk to get that return, he says. "It's a very measured risk-return management approach," Williams says. The new purpose for the front office is now linked to three primary functions; market price discovery, and for assessing liquidity in markets, and in perhaps executing the overall hedging strategy.

He concedes that not every energy company will follow this model. Some companies may have a different philosophy or experience in getting higher returns without taking larger perceived risk. However, when companies "get whacked with a large loss, they get religion pretty quickly," Williams observes.

So if the trader's star has dimmed, the CRO's star is certainly on the rise. The days of the risk manager toiling away in the background are gone. The CRO's role is now front and center in the organization. Ideally "The CRO is the individual setting capital allocations and involved in the management decisions. This individual has similar status to other senior officers and in addition to chairing the risk management committee, would be the senior management voice on broader risk issues," Williams says.

Williams illustrates the change in importance with a chart he often uses in his Boston University classes *(p.34)*.

Just a few years ago, the risk manager and his/her staff were viewed as a cost center, Williams comments. The risk management department was a control point because either the internal or external auditors said the role was needed to provide greater independence. In essence, the risk management role had a narrow mandate and was created to satisfy a requirement instead of being created to serve a key role, Williams says.

POWER MARKET RISK

"The trend is moving towards having individuals with solid risk management experience and training at the senior level," Williams says. "It doesn't matter what you call these people, they are the ones who will now need to answer to a more sophisticated market including counter-

Changing Responsibilities in Risk Practice (Courtesy: Mark Williams)		
Risk Control	**Risk Manager**	**Chief Risk Officer**
Reports *only* on an exception basis	Involved in risk/return assessments at deal development stage	Senior member of management team and Chair of Risk Committee
Calculate, monitor and report exposures	Provide ongoing risk adjusted assessment, monitoring and reporting	Key decision maker in determining company risk profile and providing ongoing guidance
Develop policies and procedures	Daily calculation of risk measurement inputs including key inputs such as volatilities and correlations	Involved in the decision of how strategic capital should be allocated or re-allocated
Conduct frequent reporting	Calculate forward curve on a daily basis	Involved in establishing criteria for trader compensation
Only participate in post-deal risk assessments	Member of the Risk Committee	Has authority to unilaterally veto transactions which are deemed too risky
Maintain an exceptions log		

parties, investment community, regulators and third-party rating agencies. Such stakeholders will want to know where the company is inherently long, where the company is short in terms of net commodity exposure, what the earnings volatility is for various time periods (e.g., monthly, quarterly), what the company's value at risk is, and what's the company's cash flow at risk. These executives will need to be well informed and very crisp in their response. That can only happen when you have a strong risk management function firmly in place," Williams believes.

"A strong risk management function used to be more of an intangible; if you had it, it was good. But you really couldn't quantify until it was too late the benefit for the company. Now, recent market defaults and sizable losses provide a timely example of why strong risk management practice and having senior people looking at risk management enhances the value of a company," Williams remarks.

Risk management credentials will be important in the future, too, and not just for the CRO. "In the next three to five years, the top energy companies (e.g., utilities) will be those which have promoted the adoption of strong risk management structure within the organization," Williams forecasts. "Actually, the most successful CFO's will be the ones that assume the joint perspective of both CRO/CFO. And I can't imagine anyone being promoted to CEO if that person doesn't have a strong grasp of risk management – risk and return relationships, measurements, strategies and implemented controls."

So much for the future. What about the here and now? To have a successful risk management group, you need to have a strong risk management culture at the top that fosters and gives credibility to the CRO, Williams remarks.

POWER MARKET RISK

The TXU Approach

Are there companies that have a strong risk management culture? You bet. One of them is TXU.

Is risk management like football? Yes, if you are G. Patrich Simpkins, executive vice president and CRO at TXU. We interviewed him at length about the risk management program at his company. In explaining risk management to his Board of Directors, Simpkins likes to use a football analogy. "A football team is on the field. The referee is the regulator. The company has the offense. The defense basically represents the market at large and your competitors. The company obviously is trying to score. The quarterback is either the head of retail sales, plant operations or trading. The coach is on the sidelines. He's the business unit president. The defensive coordinator is the head of the back office. The offensive coordinator is the head of the front office.

"Where's the risk manager? The risk manager is the guy in the booth with the microphone and all the playbooks. Before his team goes into battle, he's already reviewed his playbooks and the plays he sees the other team running. He's already done an analysis and determined the first 20 plays that the team can run. He has choices all along the way because the game's going to change, the score is going to change, and time is going to wind down. While there are unlimited choices, events limit the legitimate choices that the team has. The risk manager narrows it down to a small group of preferred choices," Simpkins says.

Further, he points out, "The team needs to know the ramifications of each choice. The risk manager is the person who is looking at the offense, the defense, and the teams on the field. He is suggesting plays to the coach based on plays he has in his book, offenses he has at his disposal, and defensive positions that could outscore the opponent. He also is there to see that it's done effectively and without causing a penalty."

However, not everyone understands the important role the CRO plays. Notes Simpkins: "At a recent dinner, I was discussing risk management with the head of an international business. He thought that the risk manager was the referee, waving the flags when somebody does something wrong. I said: 'No that's the regulator. If the risk manager is waving flags, he's not managing risk, because the risk has already occurred and the loss has already happened.'"

So if you transfer the football analogy to business, what can you learn? "It tells you that the middle office role – risk management role – is about tactics, operations, portfolio optimization of the company, and applied strategy," Simpkins comments. "By strategy, I mean giving the company options it can execute relative to the portfolio it has, the talent it can obtain or the capital at its disposal, over time, to reduce its earnings volatility and increase the company's P/E ratio as a result. Typically, P/Es are built over time as a result of consistency, not inconsistency. Trading operations that have high volatility don't have high P/E ratios.

"Let's take strategic planning. The distance between two points in a market is not a straight line. In order to go from point A to point B, risk managers must understand the portfolio and all the changes that can be made to that portfolio, given market volatility over time. That strategic part of risk management is the other half of strategic planning, which says there are numerous scenarios that portfolios can experience. If that's the case, what portfolio structure will give you the maximum net present value and the biggest return to your stakeholders over time

POWER MARKET RISK

given different market conditions?

"From a portfolio standpoint, the responsibility of the middle office and risk management is to say how the company can best optimize what it currently owns. For example, TXU has customers, generation, and trading. How do we optimize these to maximize the return relative to the risk that we take? The middle office and the CRO must understand the risk profile of its stakeholders and prospective stakeholders. That understanding has be driven down through a risk culture in the company, through policies, procedures and practices, through operations, which means keeping risk return management foremost in everyone's mind.

"Why is that important? Because, the truth is, no matter how good a middle office the company has or how good the risk manager is, if there isn't a strong risk culture, policies, practices and procedures, and a way to remind people of that in their day-to-day routine, you've already lost out. The first salesman out the door is putting shareholders' trust and the name of the company at risk if he promises to do something he can't do. Or, if he promises to do something that is delivered but it's not something the company is operationally structured to effectively manage.

"From the portfolio level, you move to the operational level. Operations is basically blocking and tackling. But how do I help my business unit president actually deliver quality earnings with a minimum amount of volatility and risk? From an operational standpoint, you have deals, transactions, acquisitions, and other actions already in your book. Therefore, risk managers look at ways to minimize or develop a dynamic hedging strategy. That's true whether it's retail, generation, or trading. It means creating a plan to manage week to week to mitigate certain risks relative to return as the company moves forward, analyzing potential impacts, and reducing risks of any negative impacts on an ongoing basis.

"The tactical level is problem resolution done on a day-to-day to day basis. It's an inquiry from FERC that must be investigated. Or, it could be the fact that you have high volatility or a correlation breakdown in the market. Because of tactical issues, a company may have to take action in the market to hedge a customer obligation or hedge a position.

"Any middle office or risk management structure that doesn't handle the strategic, portfolio, operational, and tactical view is failing in one aspect or another. I don't think that's something companies typically consider. It's usually only thought about in crisis. I think the importance of risk management is to handle risk prospectively, not retrospectively. Too often the whole discussion of risk management comes at the end, not at the beginning.

"Sometimes people ask, what do you mean by risk management? Or sometimes you might hear people in the front office saying; 'we're the ones that actually manage risk. The middle office does risk control.' When someone says that I always give him or her an analogy involving a trader. The trader realizes that in order to make his earnings numbers and the company's numbers he needs to do one more trade. He also realizes that he has enough risk capital to make it. But he realizes that his risk return tradeoff is not appropriate or nearly as high as the averages in the portfolio or the target percentages. If you're in the front office, do you make that trade or not?

"The reality is, everyone in the front office would say to the trader, make that trade. The trader spends the risk capital, makes the number, makes his earnings, and gets his bonus. But, someone in the middle office would appropriately tell the trader that the risk/return ratio for that transaction degrades the rest of the portfolio, and on a long-term value basis, the trader shouldn't make that trade.

"Risk management really falls in the middle office. Risk exploitation falls in the front office. Collecting and accounting for risk falls in the back office. Everyone should be focused on risk/return management, not just risk management and return management. And if that's true, then the middle office should be focused more on risk/return optimization than it is on the risk controls, limits, policies and procedures. Companies must have those, and they are cornerstones to good risk management. But that's not risk management, it's risk control or risk practice. Companies need those rules to be successful. But that's the minimum ante in order to play. It's what you do with all of that information and whether or not you have the right transparency, metrics and reporting that help drive decisions. That's really risk management," Simpkins says.

Chapter 4

A Quick Look at Futures, Derivatives, and Indices

Managing risk means transferring that risk so that the company isn't bearing its full weight. When handling market risk, transferring risk or hedging means offsetting risk with various financial instruments. The types of instruments generally used in power markets are exchange-traded instruments such as futures contracts and options, over-the-counter and futures derivatives, and price indices. In some markets like weather, companies also use insurance policies to hedge risk.

There is a significant difference between speculating in a market and using a market to manage risk. A speculator takes a position, hoping for financial gain. A company using futures or derivatives to manage risk wants to protect itself from an adverse action in the market. Therefore, it will choose the hedging instruments that suit its portfolio and its management philosophy.

It is the Chief Risk Officer's role to make certain that the company's position is protected at all times. If senior management has developed clear guidelines and if all those involved in executing the company's risk activities understand and abide by those guidelines, then a company will be making informed hedging choices.

A trading group or "front office" executes trades in order to hedge a position. Traders make decisions based on fundamentals in the market such as supply and demand and on technical indicators. The market risk group in the risk management program monitors the trades to see that trading positions conform to company policies, and that the trades are offsetting the company's risk. There must be oversight in order to have an effective trading group. In situations where there have been 'rogue' traders, oversight has been lacking or non-existent (for more on that, see our chapter on the trader mentality). Don't let that happen to you.

The Futures Market

Futures and options markets are regulated markets that provide a number of economic benefits. The Commodity Futures Trading Commission (CFTC), the federal regulatory agency for futures trading, identifies the following benefits:

- With many potential buyers and sellers competing freely, futures trading is a very efficient means of determining the price level for a commodity. This is commonly referred to as price discovery.
- Futures markets permit producers, processors, and users of commodities, debt instruments and currency markets a means of passing the price risks inherent in their businesses to traders who are willing to assume these risks. In other works, commercial users of the markets can hedge, which is to enter into an equal and opposite transaction in order to reduce the risk of financial loss due to a change in price and, by doing

so, lower their costs of doing business. This results in a more efficient marketing system and, ultimately, lower costs for consumers; and
- Since futures markets are national or worldwide in scope, they act as a focal point for the collection and dissemination of statistics and vital market information.

An active futures market, the CFTC points out, will create a tremendous demand by traders for information. "Futures exchanges tend to become collection centers for statistics on supplies, transportation, storage, purchases, exports, imports, currency values, interest rates, and other pertinent information. These data, which are compiled and distributed throughout the exchange community on a continuous basis, are immediately reflected in the trading pits as traders digest the new information and adjust their bids and offers accordingly."

With active selling and buying of futures, "the market determines the best estimate of today's and tomorrow's prices for the underlying commodity."

Because prices are determined in an open and competitive process, the Commission says these prices "are considered to be accurate reflections of the supply and demand for a commodity, and for this reason they are widely used as today's best estimate of tomorrow's cash market prices for a standardized quantity of a commodity."

Price discovery is also an important function of a futures market. "Price discovery is the process of arriving at a figure at which one person will buy and another will sell a futures contract for a specific expiration date. In an active futures market, the process of price discovery continues from the market's opening until its close," explains the CFTC. Wide participation by buyers and sellers in the

POWER MARKET RISK

futures markets lessens the opportunity for control by one side or the other. "Because they are freely and competitively determined, futures prices are generally considered to be superior to administered prices or prices that are determined privately."

Futures contracts are standardized for quantity, quality and location so buyers and sellers bargain only over price. Further, since futures prices are key reference points and since cash markets are often affected by the same factors impacting futures markets, cash and futures markets tend to increase and decrease together.

Energy markets and price movements are uncertain. A hurricane in the Gulf of Mexico can cause natural gas production to be shut down, sending prices for natural gas higher. Demand for electricity may soar during the summer, sending electricity prices higher. The Commission explains, "while there is no way to eliminate uncertainty, futures markets provide a competitive way for commodity producers, merchandisers, processors, and other who may own the actual commodity to transfer some price risk to speculators who will willingly assume such risk in hopes of making a profit."

The process of hedging involves the concurrent use of both cash and futures markets. Hedging can help the cash market work better since hedging stretches the marketing period, protects inventory values, and permits forward pricing of products.

The purpose of futures is to discover a forward price for a commodity and to lessen the risk of ownership of that commodity. Futures generally aren't a way of transferring ownership of a commodity, however, since most futures transactions are settled in cash rather than settled on delivery.

Futures market movements don't cause cash market prices to rise and fall. Although cash markets respond to

POWER MARKET RISK

the same factors that influence the futures market, cash markets are often affected by regional factors. For instance, gasoline futures may be descending on the New York Mercantile Exchange, which trades a contract based on delivery to New York Harbor. But if there is a refinery problem in California, gasoline prices on the West Coast may be rising since local supply will be affected by the refinery problem.

There are a number of exchanges offering futures and options contracts related to the power markets in the US. The New York Mercantile Exchange (NYMEX) offers futures contracts on crude oil, gasoline, heating oil, natural gas, electricity, propane and coal. The Chicago Mercantile Exchanges offers weather futures and options contracts.

Derivatives

What is a derivative? A derivative is "a financial instrument, traded on or off an exchange, the price of which is directly dependent upon (in other words, 'derived from') the value of one or more underlying securities, equity indices, debt instruments, commodities, other derivatives instruments, or any agreed upon pricing index or arrangement," notes the CFTC. "Derivatives involve the trading of rights or obligations based on the underlying product, but do not directly transfer property. The are used to hedge risk or to exchange a floating rate of return for fixed rate of return."

Options traded on the futures market are derivatives. However, an over-the counter (OTC) derivative is one custom tailored to suit the needs of the two parties. This is one of the advantages of OTC derivatives: if a company needs specific elements in order to hedge its risk, a OTC derivative can be developed to have those elements. While options traded on a futures market are regulated,

POWER MARKET RISK

OTC derivatives aren't. Therefore, OTC derivatives have more inherent credit risk than a derivative traded on a futures exchange.

Case Study: Weather Futures on the CME

Weather futures contracts are one type of derivative that is traded on an exchange. Unlike many futures or derivatives contracts, weather deals are a way of hedging volumetric risk, not price risk.

Weather futures began trading in September 1999 when the CME launched the first exchange-traded, temperature-related futures contracts for heating degree days (HDD). The exchange initially listed HDD index futures for four U.S. cities - Atlanta, Chicago, Cincinnati, and New York. Both a futures contract and an option on futures contract were offered.

Much has changed in the weather futures market during the last three years. As of September 2002, the CME offers HDD as well as cooling degree days (CDD) futures contracts. The number of cities has grown to 10 - Atlanta, Chicago, Cincinnati, Dallas/Fort Worth, Des Moines, Las Vegas, New York, Philadelphia, Portland, OR, and Tucson. But, it's not just a case of the Exchange adding cities and contracts.

When the HDD contract was launched in 1999, the contract was slightly ahead of its time. Weather derivatives had just begun to be traded and the weather market had barely started. The weather OTC market was not ready for futures back in 1999. So, it was "tough to support a derivative when the core market wasn't established," comments Felix Carabello, Associate Director, Industrial Commodities, for the CME. Originally, the HDD contract was traded electronically, and brokers were insufficiently utilized in creating liquidity. In addition, the

CME faced competitive pressure from other online services, which were trading weather derivatives. As a result, the contract floundered.

Realizing that the weather risk industry had grown sufficiently to support exchange-traded derivatives, the CME decided to rethink its approach to the weather market, Carabello says. First of all, the CME talked to companies active in the weather market to see if a need for weather futures truly did exist and to garner support from key industry participants. The Exchange learned that yes, industry trends could now support an exchange-traded derivative contract

The question remained: How could the market best be served? The CME decided to approach the industry as a customer itself, Carabello notes. The Exchange concentrated on "delivering a viable marketplace," rather than merely a futures contract. "We look at the marketplace as a complex organism," Carabello observes. To that end, the CME made other changes. The CME opened up market access by allowing block trading. It started a Lead Market Maker program, which improved liquidity and enabled bids and offers to be continuously available. The Lead Market Maker is Wolverine Trading. All in all, the CME tried to match the trading behavior of the industry. Rather than trying to awkwardly fit the industry to the contract, the contract now suits the industry. "Now it's like putting clothes on that fit," comments Carabello.

What's ahead? The CME would like to expand the market to include a broader customer base. After all, "the holy grail is risk transference outside of your industry," remarks Carabello.

He points out that many industry sectors are driven by the weather and companies need to manage it. However, anyone trading a weather product needs to know exactly what his or her risk management objective is. For risk managers and their companies, an exchange-traded futures contract continues to have a number of benefits, especially for the risk averse. Like any futures contract, counterparty risk is minimized since trades are cleared by the Exchange and are regulated. In addition, the market has broadened so combination weather contracts can be traded as well as cross-margin trades between CME weather contracts and commodity contracts on the New York Mercantile Exchange. While some traders contend that you don't need to use an exchange because you can trade over-the-counter and not pay a broker's fee, Carabello cautions that with any trade "there's always a cost."

Price indices

Price indices are another tool used in hedging. A number of trade publications like Platt's, Bloomberg, Energy Argus, and others have price assessments that are used in the market. In fact, some standardized contracts tend to use price indices from these independent publications for the pricing basis of the deal. Generally, journalists at the publications survey participants in the market and then derive a price index for the publication based on various criteria. Methodologies between publications may vary and anyone using a published index from a trade publication should take the trouble to research the criteria used by the publication. Most publications have written methodologies and are quite clear about how prices are determined. Generally, the journalists on the publications are willing to discuss the methodologies.

A simple rule: do your research and understand the approach underlying the price index you are using before you do the deal. It's too late to do research once the deal has been struck and you find that you didn't completely understand the methodology for the price index.

Chapter 5

Market Risk Essentials

The management of market risk isn't a new phenomenon. Companies trade futures and derivatives to manage risk. However, we've just been through a turbulent period when profit, not risk mitigation, was the driving force behind market decisions. When that happens, risks increase.

If we want to establish a solid risk management program for market risk, we need to focus on oversight and governance. That's the message from The Group of Thirty, a private, nonprofit international group made up of senior representatives from the private and public sectors and academia whose mission is to explore economic and financial issues, undertook a comprehensive study of derivatives. At the time the study was done, Paul Volcker, former chairman of the Federal Reserve Board, was the chairman of The Group.

The Group published a seminal report in July 1993 entitled, *Derivatives: Practices and Principles* that gave twenty recommendations to help companies "manage derivatives activity and continue to benefit from its use." While the report focuses on risk management for companies using financial derivatives or energy derivatives, The Group of Thirty study offers solid advice on management and oversight for all companies.

The report focuses on over-the-counter (OTC) derivatives – those instruments that are customized to suit the customer or end user's needs — and disregards the futures market since that is regulated through the Commodity Futures Trading Commission.

The Group of Thirty defines a derivative transaction as "a contract whose value depends on (or 'derives' from) the value of an underlying asset, reference rate, or index." Derivatives are important, the study says, because of the role the instrument plays in giving end-users "new ways to understand, measure, and manage financial risk." Derivatives can help increase returns and save costs while giving end-users a more extensive range of tools to use for funding and investment.

Since OTC derivatives are customized transactions, risks are often assembled in complex ways, the study points out. "This can make the measurement and control of these risks more difficult and create the possibility of unexpected loss." Therefore, The Group of Thirty strongly suggests that those involved in the derivatives market – whether end-users or dealers – "should continue laying a strong foundation of good management practice. "

To assist in creating this strong foundation, The Group of Thirty made twenty recommendations to help dealers and end-users. (The report doesn't assign the terms 'dealers' and 'end-users' to any particular institutions; rather the report refers to the roles played by institutions or companies. For instance, a large energy concern could be a dealer of derivatives as well as an end-user.)

The main recommendations from the study are these:

- Determine at the highest level of policy and deci-

sion making the scope of involvement in derivatives activities and policies to be applied.
- Value derivatives positions at market, at least for risk management purposes.
- Quantify market risk under adverse market conditions against limits; perform stress simulations; and forecast cash investing and funding needs.
- Assess the credit risk arising from derivatives activities based on frequent measuring of current and potential exposure against credit limits.
- Reduce credit risk by broadening the use of multi-product master agreements with closeout netting provisions and by working with other participants to ensure legal enforceability of derivatives transactions within and across jurisdictions.
- Establish market and credit risk management functions with clear authority, independent of the dealing function.
- Authorize only professionals with the requisite skills and experiences to transact and manage the risks, as well as to process, report, control, and audit derivatives activities.
- Establish management information systems sophisticated enough to measure, manage, and report the risks of derivatives activities in a timely and precise manner.

Let's take a closer look at these recommendations. The first two set the stage for a robust risk management structure, and the remaining recommendations address the practices used by a good risk management group.

First and foremost, The Group of Thirty believes that senior management has a major role to play in governing risk management and derivatives. The board of directors of a company should approve risk management and capi-

POWER MARKET RISK

tal policies, which should be defined clearly "including the purpose for which these transactions are to be undertaken." Additionally, senior management should approve all controls and procedures to implement these policies. Managers at all levels are expected to enforce the policies.

Markets change and, therefore, policies should change. The report suggests that senior management plan for periodic review of the risk management and capital policies to make certain they continue to meet the needs of the market and the company.

The Group recommends that companies "should have a market risk management function, with clear independence and authority, to ensure that the following responsibilities are carried out:

- The development of risk limit policies and the monitoring of transactions and positions for adherence to these policies.
- The design of stress scenarios to measure the potential impact of market conditions, however improbable, that might cause market gaps, volatility swings, or disruptions of major relations, or might reduce liquidity in the face of unfavorable market linkages, or credit exhaustion.
- The design of revenue reports quantifying the contribution of various risk components and market risk measures such as value at risk.
- The monitoring of variance between the actual volatility of portfolio value and that predicted by the measure of market risk.
- The review and approval of pricing models and valuation systems used by front and back-office personnel, and the development of reconciliation procedures if different systems are used."

The Group comments that market risk management is typically headed by a board level or near board level executive. This is generally the case for energy and power market companies.

The role of the risk manager or chief risk officer is an active, not a passive one. As the report states, "the market risk management function acts as a catalyst for the development of sound market risk management systems, models, and procedures. Its review of trading performance typically answers the question: are the results consistent with those suggested by analysis of value at risk?"

The following recommendations emphasize the practices to be used in valuing derivatives and analyzing positions. Remember that without the independence of the chief risk manager, many of these practices will be less effective. The trading department shouldn't be responsible for risk management and oversight. A good trading department working with an independent risk management department will be better able to meet any hedging goals set by senior management.

The Group of Thirty report recommends the following practices as part of any risk management program for derivatives:

Marking to Market

Derivatives positions should be marked to market (that is, measured against current market values) on a daily basis. This is important for evaluating risk management activities. "Marking to market is the only valuation technique that correctly reflects the current value of derivatives cash flows to be managed and provides information about market risk and appropriate hedging actions," the report says.

Marking to market involves taking the derivatives positions and using current market prices to value the positions. Since prices for commodities can change radically on a daily basis, this is the only way to monitor the actual value of derivatives positions.

Market Valuation Methods

The report recommends that derivatives portfolios "should be valued based on mid-market levels less specific adjustments, or on appropriate bid or offer levels." This means valuing portfolios on the mid-point of a range, which is always sound advice. Adjustments to the mid-market levels "should allow for expected future costs such as unearned credit spread, close-out costs, investing and funding costs, and administrative costs."

Identifying Revenue Sources

Companies should measure the components of revenue regularly. The components should also be scrutinized in enough detail so that any areas of exposure can be identified. By looking at individual sources of revenue, a dealer can obtain a better understanding of the risks and returns on any derivatives activity. Components of revenue include origination revenue, credit spread revenue, and other trading revenue. In a survey of industry practices, The Group of Thirty found that many companies failed to evaluate individual components of revenue, although The Group believes it should be common practice.

Measuring Market Risk

Companies should use a consistent measure to calculate the market risk of derivatives positions on a daily basis and then compare these positions to market risk limits.

The report suggests that:

- Market risk is best measured as "value at risk" using probability analysis based upon a common confidence interval (e.g., two standard deviations) and time horizon (e.g., a one-day exposure).
- Components of market risk that should be considered across the term structure include: absolute price or rate change convexity, volatility, time decay, basis or correlations, and discount rate.

Value at Risk (VaR) is "the expected loss from an adverse market movement with a specified probability over a particular period of time."

The report gives the following example: with 97.5% probability (or confidence interval), corresponding to calculations using about two standard deviations, it can be determined than any change in portfolio value over one day resulting from an adverse market movement won't exceed a specific amount.

At the same time, there is a 2.5% probability of experiencing an adverse change in excess of the calculated amount. Use of VaR should cover all major market risk components listed in The Group's recommendations.

The one-day time horizon gives management the ability to know and decide daily on any change in the risk profile. It also is in keeping with the concept of marking to market.

Once a method of risk management has been chosen, the report says that market risk limits should be set based on factors such as: "management tolerance for low probability extreme losses versus higher probability modest losses; capital resources; market liquidity; expected profitability; trader experience; and business strategy."

POWER MARKET RISK

Stress Simulations

The Group recommends that companies routinely perform simulations to see how portfolios would perform under stress conditions. "Simulations of improbable market environments are important in risk analysis because many assumptions that are valid for normal markets may no longer hold true in abnormal markets." The simulations should take into account historical events and future possibilities. Further, the tests should look not just at the impact of price changes, but also at the impact of long periods of inactivity.

Investing And Funding Forecasts

Companies should periodically forecast the cash investing and funding requirements arising from their derivatives portfolios, The Group says. The size and nature of mismatches in investing and funding will determine how often the forecasts are performed and at what level of detail.

Practices by End-users

End-users (an energy company or financial institution) should adopt "the same valuation and market risk management practices" recommended for dealers as is appropriate for the "nature, size and complexity of their derivatives activities." The Group recommends that end-users mark to market the value of their derivatives, forecast the cash investing and funding requirements that arise from derivatives activity and establish "a clearly independent and authoritative function to design and assure adherence to prudent risk limits." In addition, end-users should develop ways to assess performance and set up control procedures appropriate for their derivative activities.

Credit, Legal, Professional Recommendations

The Group of Thirty also has recommendations for credit risk, master agreements, legal issues and professional expertise. These recommendations will be reviewed in the appropriate chapters on credit risk, legal and accounting issues, and setting up a risk management group.

A last word on mark to market

Like so many other techniques, M2M can be misused. When used properly, in the sense intended by the Group of Thirty and accounting bodies, it's a neat corrective for companies. At any given time, the M2M technique tells you what your pending trades, assets and positions are really worth.

But, when used in a cavalier fashion for valuing the current value of *future* business, all kinds of things can go wrong. This is no better illustrated by some activities of Enron. Not all of these were strictly in the power or energy business – remember, Enron's *hubris* led it to portray itself as the 'world's leading company' – but some were. Enron would take a deal that might extend five or ten years into the future, and place a value on it by M2M techniques. Perhaps it would be fairer to say 'fake M2M techniques.' Many of the deals were in totally illiquid commodities or services (such as telecom bandwidth, or complex swaps), where it is impossible to determine much more than the price on the day in question. But, with the collaboration of auditor Arthur Andersen, it would price the future value of deals on a 'curve,' its estimate of the way the market and the value of the asset would progress in the future.

Even if this were done with saint-like honesty, it would be a perilously dangerous process. What five-year business projection does not become the subject of ironic grins and intracompany humor within a fairly short period of time?

To price some vaguely comprehended, illiquid commodity ten years out is merely to engage in science fiction or wishful thinking. And of course, the 'curve' came from the department in question – who else would have a clue about the forward value of something obscure, in a developing market? The final piece of the puzzle comes from an understanding of Enron's corporate culture. It was driven by bonuses rather than salaries, and by a draconian system in which 'under-performing' staff were disposed of. Every reason, then, for such 'M2M' prices to reflect huge gains, heady optimism about future markets, and the promise of fat bonuses for business unit managers. To call such practices 'smoke and mirrors' would be charitable. Smoke is relatively tangible in comparison.

Chapter 6:

What You Need To Know About The Trading Culture

A risk manager isn't a trader. But traders are a necessary part of the risk management equation. Someone has to make the trades.

When a company embarks on a risk management program, there should be a separate trading group to do the actual trades. Establishing a trading group means venturing into foreign territory for many companies. Trading can be done conservatively, and some companies may find that more to their liking. But all trading does involve risk. That should be clearly understood.

The 'Trader Mentality'

One of the forces that places a great stress on the practice of risk management is what we will call, for shorthand purposes, 'the trader mentality.' It defies simple definition, but we will explain its origins, attributes, and pitfalls before offering some solutions to the problems that it causes.

Risk-taking is endemic in human nature. In their spare time, many people skydive, drive rally cars, jump horses and do all manner of things that are sta-

POWER MARKET RISK

tistically more dangerous than sitting in a deckchair or walking in the park. Risk-taking in everyday life only becomes dangerous when pushed to extremes, or when the need for 'thrills' becomes a compulsion.

In business, we also accept risks, by the very nature of what we do. Will that company still be there when it's time for the check to clear? Will a hurricane hit land and damage a refinery? Is a record snowfall going to send electricity prices through the roof in Buffalo? Will a partner renege on a supply deal and leave you scurrying to cover your requirements? Many events like these can be covered, to a great extent, by risk management. Those that aren't – called 'pure risk' or 'naked risk,' and including natural disasters, plants failures, etc. – are covered, one would hope, by carefully selected purchases of insurance.

But what happens when human factors come into play? What do you do when a 'rogue trader' – and they do exist – starts to speculate with your funds, either for personal gain (less commonly than folklore has it) or in an attempt to cover up previous bad bets?

Your business may or may not require you to use typical 'trader' types. If you are a large utility, your risk management operations may be performed wholly or in part by skilled financial staff, or by specialists in such fields as futures or physical commodities. If you are a brokerage or trading company, the opposite is likely to be true: you are going to rely on people with a trading background to carry out your buying and selling.

In either case, you obviously aspire to employ traders who are not reckless or dishonest. Your human resources policy ought to focus on watching for the signs of 'rogue trading', which may still be attempted, even though you think you have built all the necessary systems and checks to prevent it. You should also go to considerable lengths to review new staff hiring decisions, to make sure you don't inherit someone else's known problem cases. It's not a matter of turning your company into a Police State, with unwarranted surveillance: it's a simple issue of business survival, as we have seen, time and again.

The Conventional Wisdom Of Trading

What do good traders do? They accept that you have to put money on the table to play, but they don't take unrealistic actions. Good traders can usually recite a mantra of golden rules, many of which are true, under the right circumstances:

In a falling market, *the first loss is always the smallest one*. Meaning, it's better to sell and get out rather than to hold on, praying for recovery and incurring bigger losses. Your trading horizon is of finite length: you're not betting on returns over decades, you're seeking to counter adverse market trends on a shorter timescale, weeks or months. It's therefore very risky to 'double your bets' in defiance of trends, without thoroughly evaluating the increased risk. This 'first loss' rule, then, is a pragmatic one that can save you untold headaches, if you are risk-averse.

Similarly, *Don't 'fight the tape'* by taking short positions against a rising market. When buyers outnumber sellers, markets rise. And when sellers outnumber buyers, prices fall. It's self-evident, and it's true! Even if the logic of a price move is not readily apparent, don't bet on 'fundamentals' to rescue you in a reasonable time frame. Some of the longest faces you will see are those of players who have bet against a general market trend. Think of short sellers during the 1998-2000 stock market boom. In the long term, they were 'right.' In the short term, they suffered.

'You're only as good as your last trade': Meaning, don't get delusions of grandeur when you have a little luck, or think that you're a halfwit when some unexpected reversal occurs. Traders need self-confidence, but not arrogance, to succeed.

You don't have to play every hand: Meaning, when markets are chaotic or trading volume is thin, there's no duty on your part to contribute liquidity in the form of substantial dollars. You can test the waters to see whether reported market prices are true, but you don't have to commit major money to do this.

Test your theories: Meaning, if there's a rumor that you believe (did you try to verify it?), then experimentally take a position that reflects your assessment of the market trend. But don't bet the farm on it.

Avoid over-theorization: Meaning, don't get locked into forecasts of business cycles, oil prices rises or collapses, or some fad the business press has just identified. Here one might think of the fanciful 'wave' theories of long-term market behavior. Respond as you need to in such circumstances, but don't start to believe that there are secret, inexorable laws at work that must fulfill themselves. Maybe there are, but betting money on them will contradict one of the above rules, which derive from practical experience and not from theory.

Gurus and mavens don't know anything you don't know: Meaning, if they were so smart, they'd be placing their own bets and getting very rich, very quietly, not sharing their advice with you.

Stealth trading is clever trading. If you need to buy or sell large positions, do you give the game away? Do outsiders always see you coming? Don't get the reputation of being a 'market mover.' It's good for the ego, but long-term, bad for the company's treasury.

All of these rules contain a germ of truth. What about those who ignore them? For lack of a better word, these are the 'bad' or 'unlucky' traders. The results are the same, in the end.

There's a sub-set of rules that relate to trading as practiced by utilities. Here, the rate of 'churn' is apt to be much lower, and trading conducted in a more strategic form, aside form the necessity to cover short-term operating issues.

Don't get twitchy. Not every market move presages a new trend, and not every blip in prices needs to be addressed. If your risk management group has set the right goals, and constructed hedging properly, you only need to start reacting as critical points are reached.

Be ultra-cautious with options, swaps and derivatives. As the folksong 'House Of The Rising Sun' says: "they've been the ruin of many a poor man ..." A great deal of care needs to be taken before taking positions in complex instruments, simply because the number of things that can go wrong rises exponentially with the number of factors built in.

Bad Trading

What do bad traders do? Well, first, you should realize that the Darwinian forces in the market very quickly shake the very bad traders out, on to the sidewalk, or on to an unsuspecting new employer. There's one possible way of recognizing that type: They'll have resumes that are far too busy.

POWER MARKET RISK

Borderline bad traders behave like suckers at the casino. There, you see marks double their bets, bet on 'red' because it's lucky, never draw against inside straights ... except their rationale is different. In a casino, the odds are *always* against the player, and in favor of the house. In free markets, of sufficient liquidity, you stand to see something more akin to a zero-sum game being played. But the borderline trader comes in with grandiose thoughts of 'geopolitical strategy,' or 'contrarianism' or 'waves,' or what the *Farmer's Almanac* says about next winter ... and bit by bit, steadily loses more money than he gains.

What you want, however, for your risk management strategy is something close to the zero-sum game. Win a little, lose a little, but don't bet the business. The aim of risk management, as we've said in many different ways, is to manage risk, not increase it!

How Busy-ness Can Go Wrong

Once upon a time, trading was conducted through personal contact, usually by phone, sometimes over lunch or drinks. A deal was a deal; a price was something agreed on. Without any intent to suggest 'those were the days,' things have changed a lot! While some business will still take place in the old-fashioned way – and deals may be finalized with a call – it's increasingly common for deals in both futures and physical markets to originate from screen-based activity.

This has been a developing phenomenon since NYMEX and other exchanges launched futures markets in the 1980s. And it has taken off in a huge way since the early 1990s, with trading arenas open for all manner of financial instruments, derivatives and commodities. In general, this has been economically beneficial. Markets generally run better when price information and product availability is transparent, rather than the subject of rumor or hearsay, and when transactions can be speedily concluded in a financially secure fashion.

But there is a downside in trader behavior. It's what we'll call, for lack of an accepted term, the 'Game Boy syndrome.' It really is easy for a trader to become mesmerized by the constant flow of data on two, three, four or more real-time screens posing tempting options for buying and selling throughout the working day.

If you are a *trading* company, you probably want to hire folks with the patience and concentration to sift through fast-changing market opportunities and jump on deals. After all, trading companies make their money by being fleet of foot, quick with decisions, and oriented towards the occasional gamble. If you are any other type of company, you will want to make sure that you harness trading activity to your *strategy* and not merely to evanescent opportunities. Certainly, that's what your Risk Management people ought to be saying. Don't let trading develop a 'life of its own.' And be cautious of how you deploy traders who seem to have such a compulsion.

Horror Stories

Rather than generalize, let's look at some infamous tales of trading mishaps. Most of them involve well-meaning individuals and companies, rather than out-and-out crooks. But the outcome is still the same. Put simply, the result of badly conceived trading practices, sloppy oversight, or poor risk management procedures is *ruin.*

Don't be deceived by the fact that only a few of

these examples directly concern energy trading, or the power industries. With the increasingly commoditization of power, and with the advent of deregulation, the kind of goofs perpetuated in markets for financial instruments and commodities can happen quite easily in energy markets. In fact, one of the most visible companies to step on a banana peel was Enron, which developed the viewpoint that it could 'trade anything,' according to a similar set of rules. Its downfall stemmed from a number of converging factors, but it's our view that the company's trading practices and underlying business philosophy was setting it up for an eventual fall, long before financial jiggery-pokery with 'off balance sheet' entities finally raised Wall Street awareness of its precarious position.

Barings

It's the stuff of a TV docudrama or a Hollywood film – and it became both. A bright young English trader, Nick Leeson, begins wowing his managers with a daring strategy of speculation in financial futures out of Baring's Singapore office. The old-line, conservative banking business has not seen returns like it, and ascribes it to brilliant trading, and – as always – the emergence of a 'new set of rules' in a globalizing, fast-moving business. An old-school-tie type of senior executive was quoted as saying: "I haven't got a clue how he does it, but the profits are fantastic."

In reality, what was happening was something quite different. Set limits on exposure were being ignored, and risking trades in financial futures were being made. While some deals resulted in spectacular profits, others did not. The evidence was obfuscated thanks to poor oversight. Only when a particularly dismal set of bets was placed on Japan's Osaka futures market did the first cracks appear. Investigation showed that the trader – unaccountably, working alone – had committed nearly all of the bank's capital to positions that could not be unwound in time to prevent disaster. Leeson went to jail, and Barings vanished into the Netherland's ING Bank.

What could have been done better? Oversight was clearly missing, and in a big way. As well as better understanding Leeson's strategy, management should have strictly enforced rules on trading limits.

Enron

Entire books will be written about Enron in years to come. And we treat some of its mistakes separately at various points in this book. But the underlying thesis of Enron's collapse was another attack of *hubris,* and yes, belief in a 'new set of rules.' In this case, the rules were ones Enron wrote for itself. Seeing that its origins in natural gas pipelining and marketing – with a few chemical operations on the side – did not fit the magic mantra of high returns, the company re-invented itself. As a trader in gas and electricity, but also as a cogenerator of power, a 'global utility,' a trader in commodities, water, financial instruments, even evanescent quantities like 'bandwidth.' Business boomed. Imitators appeared. After all, how could you stand by and watch such a heralded success story in a stodgy industry, and not want to be a player yourself? Enron's competitors were offshoots of other oil and gas companies with a similar gleam in their eyes, and worried by the strategic threat of an 'assetless' company owning the playing field.

Enron did some things right. It realized that

POWER MARKET RISK

some kind of open exchange was needed for such trades, and built one, in the form on Enron Online.

It also decided – details are murky, but the outcome is not – that it needed to find ways of financing risky moves in a less readily apparent fashion, plus find ways of burying 'boring' under-performing businesses and other business flops, away from the balance sheet. Thus a web of interlocking subsidiaries grew, covering up the company's true financial position. Stock market valuations soared, because Wall Street saw Enron as a model of the 'new economy,' every bit as exciting as the 'dot com' companies of the late 1990s.

When the first few cracks in the edifice appeared, reality was denied. It took a steady deluge of bad news and dismal revelations to finally bring the company to its knees. And we still don't know more than a part of the story.

The impact of Enron's fall on power markets is quite clear. First, it removed one of the most active players from the markets. Second, post-event forensics have raised powerful suspicions (and, increasingly, objective proof) that all was not as it seemed with California's power market price bubbles in 2000-2001, and that the fog of deregulation had been used by Enron and others to turn a fast buck by 'wash' trades, 'roundtripping' and other unethical, and perhaps illegal, stunts.

In this case, Enron itself, rather than individuals, was the 'rogue trader.'

Enron's trading business is now owned by UBS Warburg, whose management has not been seen dancing with joy at the outcome of the pricey acquisition.

What could have been done differently? First, Enron's senior management should have distinguished between the realistic and the impossible. Second, they should have promoted a less rapacious corporate culture, with its emphasis on winning at all costs. Third, they should have believed in – and enforced – their own risk management and ethical codes. Fourth, investors and analysts should not have been fooled by the 'new economy' propaganda from Enron and other companies. Fifth, bankers should not have extended so much credit to the organization, nor participated in some many of its dubious 'off balance sheet financing' schemes. Sixth, the company's lawyers and auditors should have done their jobs, and insisted on a higher standard of financial probity. Seventh, the board should have woken up and taken notice, instead of sleeping through the whole affair. The list could be extended, but clearly, Enron's failure can be blamed on a whole raft of reasons.

Allied Irish Bank

At Allied Irish Bank, it was 'only about money.' But the scandal that washed over its US subsidiary was all about risk management. A single trader there – perhaps helped by a blind eye turned by counter parties – regularly exceeded his trading limits in a losing battle to cover up some earlier losses in currency markets, for several years. By the time the chickens came home to roost, AIB was out $700 million.

What could have been done differently? This case is clearly one of flawed oversight and enforcement of trading limits.

'War stories' like these tend to provoke the reaction 'ah, but it can't happen here!' Maybe so. But that's what the managements of these noble entities said, too. Somehow, risk management failed. Sometimes

POWER MARKET RISK

because of a 'rogue trader' – though they are far fewer in number than folklore would have us believe – but in other cases because a company decided to ignore risk management practices, even though it theoretically had them in place. That's the most dangerous situation of all, when a company turns 'rogue.'

G. Patrich Simpkins, Executive VP AND CRO at TXU comments: "If you looked at all the recent energy and non-energy company failures and did it on an impact to P/E ratio, share price, income basis, in very rare circumstances is the failure caused by a rogue trader. If it is a rogue trader, it's not a market risk. It's an operational risk."

Chapter 7

How Well Do You Know This Guy, Really? Human Issues in Risk Management

We've looked at the 'trader mentality' and the human side of risk management in Chapter 6. With those thoughts in mind, here are some strategies for avoiding problem traders or risk employees, and the upsets they can bring.

The Interview

You'll be placing a lot of trust, and real money, in the hands of your traders – and other risk management personnel. Select then as carefully as you would a new CFO!

That means, multiple interviewing. Have several senior people interview the candidate. Do it on separate days, to see if he or she can 'maintain the pose.' Always hold second interviews if you're not sure. Make sure that your interviewers follow some basic rules of interviewing, and remind them what they are if they've forgotten: like, read the resume, and figure out your questions in advance. Be politically correct, but don't be afraid to ask questions that are legal and ethical.

Traders, by the nature of their business, are always quite impressive in person. Like realtors, stockbrokers and senior sales people, their demeanor and appearance is 50% or more of their professional 'toolkit.' You should expect to be impressed, or there's something wrong already.

However, you should not be bamboozled.

We have known many oil traders who are movie-star handsome, and dress in the epitome of taste. At least one went to jail.

Ask The Right Questions

In a thirty-minute interview, you have to get to the story behind the resume and the smiling face. Here are some probing questions that will get you closer to understanding this person. Although you have to explain the job to some extent, you shouldn't be speaking for more than a few minutes. You should be listening to answers, and understanding the motivations of the candidate's questions.

Why did you leave your last job, or *why are you interested in changing jobs?* Look for a plausible answer: 'looking for a job with more responsibility,' or 'looking for a new challenge' are clichés, but neutral answers. 'They're downsizing' begs the question – in your mind – *why are they getting rid of you, particularly?* (Find a diplomatic way to ask it).

If applicable, *why have you had so many jobs?* Face it, in today's economy, with waves of takeovers and corporate reorganizations, 'tree-huggers' are less common than they used to be. 'Job-hopping' is not the disgrace it once was. To progress, people need to move, on occasion. Similarly, in 'two-job' families, people will often need follow a better-paid or more securely employed spouse to a different city. But, there is such a thing as a 'too busy' resume. Does your candidate's past in any way suggest to you some instability, or continuing irresolution about career path? Listen carefully to the answer to this question.

Try a test question to see if you are dealing with someone who can't stick to the subject, or who has 'off-the-wall' theories: *How does the market look to you today?* If you get a fairly crisp answer, free of theory, you may feel reassured. If not, what is the drift of the answer? Ask a few more questions of the sort, paying attention to any 'hidden message' expressed in the replies.

Try an old stand-by: *What is it about risk management that attracts you?* Or, *What makes you a trader?* This may be the question that draws a neutral response, like 'it's what I do best,' or, 'I like to manage complicated, fast-changing situations.' What you should watch for is any 'buggy-eyed' response full of macho bravado.

Try a simple test: *Tell me about one of your most successful decisions.* Beautifully open-ended, this should prompt a relatively sober answer, one might hope. Again, watch carefully for any signs of a 'we really screwed them,' or 'we were really smart' kind of story.

If that doesn't work, interpose some other innocuous question – ask: *What would you say was the dumbest thing you ever did, in a risk management context?* You should expect at least some small confession of failure here, to demonstrate humility.

Be blatant, and say: *We have the feeling here that the market has suffered from games by some real sharp operators lately. The public seems to think there are a lot of crooks in this business. Would you agree?* If you get a nebulous answer, say: *'Oh? What about [insert some suitable name here]?* You're looking for a 'party line' when you ask this question. Can your candidate think for him/

herself? What are this person's perceptions, measured against the current wisdom?

The old stand-bys are always worth playing. Where did this person go to school? Where else has he/she worked? If you know people there, drop their names. *Did you study with X? Did you work with Y? Were you there when Z got the boot? Is Fred still running the Q department?* Listen for verisimilitude. Even if these people are not quoted as references, there's no reason why you should not verify your contact is 'my old buddy,' if it's claimed, with a discreet phone call.

If your candidate comes from some company with a checkered history, or one that went broke, you should definitely ask: *What happened at [Company X]? What were you doing there?* That doesn't mean you're stigmatizing people for their past associations, not in the least. But you want to be sure that your candidate was not some arch-instigator of some foolishness, don't you? Or whether this person is very touchy or sensitive to implied criticism? Be sure you actually know what you're talking about when it comes to such past events, and keep your reactions to yourself. There's no sense in getting into a pissing match with a candidate, whatever the answer. It's bad PR.

Beware of *resume enhancement!* Think about resumes, for a moment. They vary from the dull chronological recitation of companies and positions held, to carefully crafted works that emphasize responsibilities, achievements, management skills and goals. Headhunters admit that about 10-15% of resumes they see are 'enhanced' in some fashion or another. Imaginary MBAs are a particularly common element in recent cases made public.

It doesn't matter which sort of resume you are looking

at – true or fabricated – because either is capable of containing misinformation, or romanticization. Of course, you have more ways of checking on this, but the interview is a good time to ask questions that help detect any falsification.

If there is a conspicuous date gap: Ask, politely: *What were you doing between 1994 and 1996?* You need to know! Was this maternity leave, a gap to take an MBA, was your candidate you out of work, or was it a trip to the country club penitentiary?

Beware of weasel words and jargon: Resumes are full of claims like 'responsible for $xxMM in activity' and 'implemented new systems.' Okay, then ask: *Who had the final decision on activities, above $1MM (or whatever)? What does this 'system upgrade' mean in dollar terms, capital budget, or annual savings? How many people reported to you? Who did you report to? How many other traders (or whatever) were there? What, specifically, did you do, on a day-to-day basis? Describe a typical day to me ...* All of these facts are verifiable to a great extent, and you should expect no difference in your independent findings and the candidate's response.

The candidate's own questions will reveal a lot. Make a note of them as you go. Of course, you'll be asked about salary, about a title, job responsibility, reporting lines, benefits, all the usual stuff. Don't spend ages explaining it all: some more lowly HR person can give the person the full 'benefits and policies' package, and answer those questions. But what about the other questions? The way they are phrased, the content, the body language all speak: and they are all quite revealing.

Remember, the idea of interviewing is to get to the truth, not to make friends with your candidate, or to talk about golf. This is one – perhaps the best – of your chances to find out how he/she ticks.

However, it's not your only way. You're going to compare your interview notes with the other interviewers. And you're going to listen to comments – positive or negative – raised by your HR professionals, who will have pre-screened the candidate. Aren't you?

HR Interviews

You really do need to make sure that someone with a dispassionate view of the hiring process sees *all* candidates, whatever the position. However smart you think you are at spotting 'lemons' and 'winners,' human resource pros see more candidates in a day than you do in a month, unless you're in the middle of some firestorm of staff replacement. The instincts of good HR folk – and we are presuming that this is the only kind you employ – can bring out facts that you have neglected, or reveal interesting character insights.

In addition, you can have the HR people take care of any initial explanations of corporate culture, purpose, etc. They are the ones who should tell candidates that there is a strict code of business ethics, and an agreement to abide by it that they will have to sign, for example. It doesn't hurt if you also make this point, of course.

We would hope that your code of conduct extends to employees' stock portfolios, and frowns upon ownership of stock in companies with which you do significant business, or compete.

You may also ask this question, but the HR folks are the ones to say: *What do you know about us?* Anyone worth employing will at least know your line of business, have read the annual report, and can recall a couple of recent press stories about the company.

There's no excuse for a candidate not having checked out that much about you on the Internet, at home or a public library. So, watch here for fulsome praise, or half-witted questions.

Headhunters & Consultants

How are you finding your candidates? Just from display ads in newspapers or magazines? Via the Internet? Do they just appear in the mail, as random resumes? Do other employees refer them to you? There's nothing wrong with any of these routes, of course.

Chances are, for senior positions, you will either use the services of a job placement specialist, or that you will have a candidate offered to you by such people.

There are at least two types of 'headhunter' – the general purpose, and the career-specific. For your own purposes, it doesn't matter which you use, but you're probably better off with an agency or consultant which specializes in financial, accounting, or trading candidates.

Make your headhunter do some of the work! Don't put up with agencies that just unload their database on you, without screening them for characteristics and career experience that you require. Give the agency a clear briefing on what it is you want, without being so prescriptive that there are only two candidates in the entire western world. When we say don't be prescriptive, we mean, among other things: Don't disqualify candidates because they are older (it's illegal and 'career enders' are often the most loyal employees), those who seem to want too much money (maybe they'll settle for less), those who look more like Jerry Garcia than Tom Cruise, or 'used to work for Enron.'

Screen your headhunter: Ask whom they have placed recently, or who their other clients are. Chances are, they'll tell you. Ask them to do proper background checks on people they refer to you as candidates. This may seem demeaning, or even give some offense, but it's a fact that several publicly notorious CEOs have been latterly proven to be 'empty suits' or to have puffed up their resumes with false claims, imaginary qualifications or 'mistaken' memories.

Get a pre-interview briefing from the headhunter. They're going to charge you good money to conduct a search, so expect them to give you ten minutes of time. In return, relay your own first impressions to help in future searches. *Don't* spike your deck by saying something like, 'Oh, she was good, but didn't know enough about derivatives,' because, surprise, surprise, you can bet that the candidate will come back for a second interview, brimful of newly minted knowledge out of a textbook.

Finding Out More

So, you have a job candidate that you think is right for the job. You're almost convinced. Now what? Before you make any offer – which should be subject to a reference check, if you are sane – you may want to consider 'checking out the story.'

So often, companies fall down on this stage. They assign reference checks to some junior person in HR, or take for granted what they have been told.

What we're going to recommend may raise some hackles, or bring the cry of 'impossible!' But, it makes good sense. We'll back into it, to soften the shock.

When someone buys a house, with a mortgage, they cough up all manner of financial information to a lender, or group of lenders. Tax returns, permission to check credit references, you name it. And that's all for some $300-500K family home – more in some places – where the total risk to the lender is collateralized by some physical property, on which the lender has first lien. It's not much of a gamble on their part, is it? But they guard themselves well. Smart folks!

So here you are, about to offer a fairly decently paid job to someone who may have the 'keys to the car,' if the position is senior enough. Someone who could, potentially lose you millions. It therefore seems prudent to at least ask a few questions about the following – not to the candidate, but to an independent source.

If you are a large utility, you undoubtedly subscribe to one or more national credit reporting services. This is the point at which you discretely – and from within HR – run a background check. Is this just plain nosiness? No, it's not!

You need to know a little bit about whether your candidate has some eye-popping amount of credit card debt, a string of mortgages, several cars on lease or time payments, a yacht tucked away somewhere, or other hidden liabilities. In other words, what you're aiming to do – or rather have some senior HR person do for you – is to match past income history and spending behavior, and to identify any huge mismatches.

Yes, people often inherit money and have a lifestyle that exceeds what you might think possible on a couple of low-end six-figure jobs. People also put their hands in the till.

You should also have your HR people at least *try* to get some kind of reading from previous employers. It's become very difficult to obtain what might be thought of as 'negative references,' because of the risk of lawsuits for defamation. Many companies will only confirm a candidate's former employment dates and title as a result.

You can also go to the public record. A broad Nexis search may throw up your candidate's name. Especially if there is something dark in his/her past. You could also search the back files of local newspapers in towns where this person lives or lived. Or search for their e-mail address on the 'Groups.Google.com' database of Usenet groups, dating back nearly ten years. How far you decide to go should be dependent on your relative degree of suspicion, of course, and the nature of the job on offer.

But What About The Others?

If you're going to these lengths with new staff, what about the people who are already there? In general, you know something about them already, and they ought not to be transgressing, if your compliance procedures are properly tuned.

But, do watch for sudden changes in personal fortunes, lifestyles, etc. You don't have to 'spy' on your employees, but you should be at least minimally aware of their situations. If nothing is apparently wrong, then that's fine. But if you feel suspicious, look into ways of understanding them better.

It's not a question of 'prying' or 'lack of ethics' or 'running a police state.' It's to do with money. And if you feel uncomfortable with this concept, then go and buy some liability insurance against employee fraud. You may find it is more expensive than taking simple precautions.

Compensation Issues

You will pay your staff properly, of course. Both the new members, and your existing ones. If you don't have a clear picture of the compensation spectrum in the field, your HR department – perhaps with an outside compensation consultant – can quite quickly set up a benchmark study to bring you some guidelines about the right price. But make sure that you don't set up a compensation system that undermines the whole point of risk management. It's so easy to fall into the trap of giving departments financial targets, and rewarding them for exceeding them. *Don't do it with risk management staff!* You'll be setting up a scenario where gambling to increase trading profits is encouraged. You're better off pegging any 'productivity' rewards to accomplishment of non-fiscal targets, or letting these employees participate in a more general 'profit sharing' scheme involving the whole company.

Is this a theoretical concept? No. Take Enron, where huge bonuses became a new kind of entitlement for managers in trading, and undoubtedly had a great psychological effect on their behavior. Or, outside of the energy field, think of now-bankrupt telecommunications giant Global Crossing, where the end of each quarter was marked by last-minute 'deals' – the quote marks are intentional, because most were quite illusory 'spins' of fiber capacity with other firms – that pumped up profits, and of course, executive bonuses.

We're inclined to feel the same way about granting stock options. But these, at least, have a kind of neutrality underlying them, related to stock price performance of the entire company. The main problem is, they make executives focus on short-term gains rather than the long-term health and sustainable growth of the business. Some serious rethinking of stock option programs is likely to take place in the next couple of years.

We're scarcely alone in this thinking about the role of compensation packages in causing serious problems.

Mark Williams, Risk Management Expert at the Finance And Economics Department at Boston University is a critic of recent compensation concepts. There's been a lack of focus on the risk side of the risk/return equation, Williams says. "How do you measure that [lack of focus]?" asks Williams. "In the 1990s, you can look at how the compensation schemes were established. Front-office personnel were bonus-based on their individual trade book profits," and not on company portfolio profits or importantly overall company profits.

A Chief Risk Officer can help align incentive compensation programs to ensure that the focus is linked to the overall success of the company, Williams says. There was a huge misalignment in incentive compensation and we are only now finding that contributed to the problems with energy trading, he believes. In many cases, traders may have had the perverse incentive to trade volume, without a focus on net profitability, Williams says.

Chapter 8

Credit Risk: What You Don't Know Can Hurt You

Credit risk is an issue that many companies don't consider until it is too late. The power markets got hammered by credit risk during the summer of 1998 and then slammed by credit risk in 2001 and 2002. Like the proverbial 2x4 between the eyes, credit risk has forced companies to take notice of their counterparties creditworthiness as well as their own.

Let's go back to the summer of 1998 when spot market electricity price spikes resulted in the bankruptcy of a number of companies. The debacle of 1998 taught companies to undertake more vigorous credit risk management. That summer, there were a number of "sleeve" deals done where two parties who couldn't trade with each other for credit reasons had a third party act as the middleman or the sleeve. The risk falls to the company acting as the sleeve. If one company's credit is risky, however, it can affect every company involved in the deal whether a company is a direct counterparty or not.

Before the summer of 1998, some companies might not have spent much time checking out the creditworthiness of the counterparties in deals or doing the proper research on the counterparty. The belief that the company wouldn't default on an obligation may have been the only credit risk management that was done. The concept of trust is a noble idea, but trust can't prevent your company from experiencing the effects of a counterparty's default on a deal. When a deal goes bad, it hurts the revenues of your company. No manager wants to see revenues affected, especially when research and prudence may have prevented the problem.

But what about trusting those big entities like Enron that we think couldn't turn into a credit risk? Well, Enron's disintegration has taught a major lesson to the market: trust no one. Enron's credit unworthiness not only affected other companies' revenues, but also had an impact on how ratings agencies view the energy business. The inability of companies to keep a strong credit position has affected ratings. When a company's ratings are downgraded to junk status, it severely affects a company's ability to go to the capital markets for project financing. Remember that power plant you wanted to build? Well, if your rating isn't investment grade, that power plant isn't likely to be built.

If credit risk is such a straightforward and well-understood practice, how come Enron was able to hoodwink the stock market, ratings agencies, banks, insurers, partners and clients for so long?

The answer of course is 'lack of prudent suspicion.'

At this point, we only have the evidence that has come to light in the year after its Chapter 11 bankruptcy protection filing. And of course, the clear warning signs that were finally noticed during the course of 2001.

In hindsight, the problems that sank Enron were quite self-evident:
- Even while boosting its stock, many analysts remarked on the complexity of its financial transactions, and the impossibility of clearly understanding the source of the company's revenues or its

POWER MARKET RISK

debt position.
- The lack of clarity in its financial statements was apparent to anyone who took the trouble to read the company's 10Q and 10K filings.
- Common sense might have led people in that trading community, in particular, to doubt whether the stratospheric returns Enron was claiming were possible. Trading margins are typically tight – and growing tighter with electronic markets – and the sort of growth rates and revenue increases Enron claimed were quite improbable.

It's a mystery why banks didn't see this, and tighten Enron's credit. It's also a mystery why ratings agencies like Standard & Poor's and Moody's did not blow the whistle earlier. The agencies couldn't see the off-books financing activities, but some banks were actively involved in them!

One reason that counterparties and suppliers did not act is that Enron had, by taking such a dominant position in the market, become the market. It is to be hoped that similar situations will not be allowed to develop in future. But it's also to be hoped that creditors read the warning signs and act on them. A large number of companies were left holding the bag when Enron folded, and have good reason to revamp their credit risk policies and practices.

Credit risk is defined simply as a counterparty's failure to fulfill an obligation, leaving your company with a loss, either financial or physical. Credit exposure is the amount at risk at a given time in the event a counterparty defaults. Credit loss is simply the actual loss incurred due to the default. Credit risk should measure exposure, but should also look at the possibility of defaults and recovery on defaults.

A company that embarks on a risk management program likely will be doing more business with counterparties, especially if the program calls for the trading of non-exchange-based derivatives. Credit risk is mitigated when trading exchange-based futures and options since the transactions are being handled by the exchange. There are rules and regulations governing position and price limits on exchanges that are guaranteed by the associated clearinghouse. According to the New York Mercantile Exchange, there are "a sophisticated, intricate system of safeguards [that] virtually guarantees against counterparty credit risk and default."

While exchange-based contracts do have built-in protection against credit risk, many companies will need to trade non-exchange based derivatives in order to have a well-rounded risk management portfolio. It means that a company must be ever vigilant about looking at the creditworthiness of a counterparty. In trading derivatives, a company must take the research of a counterparty's creditworthiness into its own hands and set up its own safeguards. A prudent company will set up a credit risk management group as part of its risk management program in order to make certain that credit risk is minimized.

In general, credit risk management groups have the responsibility "for analyzing the creditworthiness of potential derivatives counterparties, setting limits on such exposures, and monitoring compliance with these limits," according to research done by the US General Accounting Office. One firm visited by the GAO had set up a "separate credit management department [that] had established nine categories of creditworthiness for derivatives counterparties. The officials [of the company] said that the department used these categories to set varying

POWER MARKET RISK

limits on the amount of derivatives transactions that could be made with firms in these categories. They said that the credit management department was separate from the derivatives trading departments and reported directly to this firm's senior management."

The GAO goes on to say that the companies surveyed "had established credit risk limits and systems to ensure firms' observance of the limits. Features of their credit risk-monitoring practices included using automated systems to quickly determine whether a counter a party's limit had been exceeded; checking compliance at the end of the day and directing instances of exceeded limits to management for action; and requiring traders to seek prior management approval for some transactions, such as those exceeding a certain dollar threshold."

The companies also told the GAO that: "they reduced their credit risk by conducting most of their derivatives activities with counterparties of high credit quality." Most of these counterparties had a BBB or Baa or higher credit ratings. Interestingly, the GAO says that the agency "developed information that confirms the high credit quality of most derivatives counterparties." From publicly available data, [the GAO] identified 200 firms with swap portfolios of at least $1 billion as of year-end 1991. These firms included many financial institutions and commercial firms." Of the 200 firms, "97.5% of the total $5.5 trillion of outstanding notional amount of swaps held by these firms was recorded by firms that had investment grade ratings. Only 2.5% of the total was recorded by firms with non-investment grade ratings." GAO says. "The likelihood of default losses on investment grade credit exposure is low, on the basis of historical performance," contends the GAO.

In preparing its report, *Derivatives: Practices and Principles*, the Global Derivatives Study Group of The Group of Thirty interviewed many companies involved in derivatives trading. On the basis of those interviews, the study group made four specific recommendations on credit risk and credit exposure. The recommendations covered measuring credit exposure, aggregating credit exposures, independent credit risk management, and credit enhancement. Let's take a look at these recommendations in more detail.

Credit exposure on derivatives should be measured two ways. The first is current exposure, which is defined as "the replacement cost of derivatives transactions, that is, their market value." The second is "potential exposure, which is an estimate of the future replacement cost of derivatives transactions." Potential exposure "should be calculated using probability analysis based upon broad confidence intervals (such as two standard deviations) over the remaining terms of the transactions."

In assessing credit risk, The Group says, two questions should be asked. "If a counterparty was to default today, what would it cost to replace the derivatives transaction? If a counterparty defaults in the future, what is a reasonable estimate of the future replacement cost?"

Current exposure addresses the answer to the first question. Current exposure is an evaluation of "the replacement cost of outstanding derivatives commitments." It can be a positive or a negative number. Since current exposure represents the "actual risk to a counterparty at any point in time," it is a valuable measure of credit risk.

On the other hand, potential exposure is harder to assess, The Group points out. There are many ways to calculate potential exposure. However, simulation analysis and option valuation models tend to be the two most frequently used methodologies for calculating this aspect of credit risk. According to the report, 'the analysis generally involves a statistical modeling of the effects on the value of the derivatives of movement in the prices of the underlying variables (such as interest rates, exchange rates, equity prices, or commodity prices). These techniques are often used to generate two measures of potential exposure: expected exposure and maximum or 'worst case' exposure."

For those dealers and end-users that can't justify the cost of these simulation and statistical systems, the report suggests that they create their own "tables of factors developed under the same principles. The factors used should differentiate appropriately by type and maturity of transaction and be adjusted periodically for changes in market conditions."

The Group recommends that derivatives credit exposures as well as all other credit exposures to a counterparty "should be aggregated taking into consideration enforceable netting arrangements." Further, there should be regular calculations of credit exposures and comparisons to credit limits.

In looking at a portfolio of deals with a counterparty to determine credit risk, an end-user or dealer needs to know if netting applies. "If it does, the current exposure is simply the sum of positive and negative exposures on transactions in the portfolio."

Figuring out potential exposure is more difficult. The report warns that simply taking the sum of the potential exposures of all transactions likely will "dramatically overstate the actual exposure, even if netting does not apply." A straight sum won't make adjustments for deals that offset each other or that "have peak potential exposures at different times." A more accurate way to assess potential exposure would be a calculation that simulates the entire portfolio, the report contends. Credit exposures should be calculated on a regular basis, which may be daily or weekly.

POWER MARKET RISK

In addition, all credit exposures should be measured against the limits set for credit. When these limits are met or exceeded, management should be prepared to take any action deemed appropriate for the situation.

The credit risk management function should have "clear independence and authority," The Group comments. This independent function should be responsible for "approving credit exposure measurement standards, setting credit limits and monitoring their use, reviewing credits and concentrations of credit risk, and reviewing and monitoring risk reduction arrangement."

The report recommends that dealers have credit exposures monitored by a separate, independent management group. For end-users, the credit risk management function doesn't necessarily need to be a separate group. However, the dealing or trading part of the company shouldn't handle the credit risk function. Whether separate or not, the credit risk managers should constantly review counterparty creditworthiness as well as credit limits.

In its last credit recommendation, The Group says that the "benefits and costs of credit enhancement and related risk-reduction arrangements" should be assessed. If proposed credit downgrades would "trigger early termination or collateral requirements, participants should carefully consider their own capacity and that of their counterparties to meet the potentially substantial funding needs that might result."

Credit risk reduction arrangements include "collateral and margin arrangements; third-party credit enhancement such as guarantees or letters of credit; and structural credit enhancement through the establishment of special-purpose vehicles to conduct derivatives business."

As we've seen with every aspect of risk management,

there must be a structure in place for managing the credit risk function, one that reflects a structure similar to the general risk management program. Standards and policies must be developed and agreed upon. A credit risk management group needs to be independent if it is to serve its oversight function, and limits for credit must be developed, agreed upon and closely monitored. Only then can a company be confident that it is truly mitigating its credit risk.

Andrea S. Kramer, partner at McDermott, Will & Emery, gives a short checklist for the credit risk management process. Here are her guidelines:

Credit risk elements when selecting counterparties:

- Establish a process for selection, approval and continuation of the relationship with counterparties.
- Set counterparty risk limits by individual counterparty (as notional amounts may not accurately reflect the risk of trading with a particular counterparty).
- Develop counterparty credit standards with an eye to determining creditworthiness as well as any requirements for credit enhancements, including third party guarantees, letters of credit, or collateral support of any type.
- Set risk ratings and monitor counterparty credit limits.
- Evaluate extension of credit including current credit exposure and potential credit exposure.
- Update credit limits and re-approve credit limits on a periodic basis.

POWER MARKET RISK

Credit Risk Elements When Selecting Brokers

- Use creditworthiness determination to set broker credit standards, including any requirements for third party guarantees, letters of credit, or collateral support of any type.
- Assign and monitor risk ratings.
- Determine what level of credit will be extended
- Determine margin requirements
- Draft standard contract provisions and settlement terms
- Ensure broker agrees to certification of compliance with the company's conflict of interest policies.
- Establish methodology to measure credit risk.
- Document the requirements to meet credit risk management requirements including credit support documents and mater agreements or netting agreements.
- Make certain that credit risk management reports cover credit expenses and counterparty reports.
- Require trades to be made only with pre-approved counterparties with pre-set credit limits.
- Define approval process for exceptions to credit limits.
- Specify the process for reporting and monitoring exceptions to credit limits.

Any company's credit risk management program must have clearly defined credit policies and procedures. These procedures and policies will facilitate transactions with creditworthy counterparties and prohibit transactions with counterparties whose credit is below company standards.

Documenting a company's credit risk management policies is very important in order to give the credit risk management staff clear guidelines. Equally as important, however, is that these guidelines be disseminated to traders as well because everyone in the company with a risk management role must be fully aware of all policies and procedures.

A credit risk management document "should define clear roles and responsibilities within a credit management program," say Ernst & Young's Andrew Lese and Roger Hakanson, writing in *Energy & Power Risk Management*. The document should include underwriting criteria that give a creditworthiness assessment, which in turn determines credit quality. According to Lese and Hakanson, "a scoring process assigns an internal rating to each counterparty and, based on this rating, a credit limit is allocated." The limit that is set "represents the maximum amount of acceptable credit exposure for the counterparty without another level of review."

"Netting arrangements allow the offsetting of amounts due to and from the same counterparties in the event of a default, thereby reducing the gross exposure," contend Lese and Hakanson. Credit enhancement "allows a lesser or unrated counterparty to execute transactions they would not be able to do on an unsecured basis," the authors say. Credit enhancement can be in the form of parental guarantees, letters of credit, or other financial backing. But Lese and Hakanson caution that "use of a guarantee or letter of credit requires a further credit analysis of the guarantor, as well as a review of existing credit exposure to the guarantor. "

The policies should also set down a risk measurement methodology. "Credit risk measurement is a complex process that determines the total credit exposure for a counterparty across business units and commodities," Lese and Hakanson say. The exposure must be compared to the credit limit for the counterparty in order to determine what credit is available for additional transactions.

Credit risk management policy documentation must also look at limits and how limits are structured. "An effective limit structure ensures that credit risks are maintained within a management-approved tolerance level. This must be balanced against the potential of putting unnecessary constraints on the development and execution of the business," Lese and Hakanson remark.

As part of credit risk management policies, it is important to be able to rate a counterparty for creditworthiness. The GAO looked at investment grade companies, for the most part. But in the energy business, not every company involved in power markets is big enough to be rated by Standard & Poor's or Moody's Investor Service. It becomes necessary for a company to create its own ratings for counterparties.

Credit scoring potential counterparties is the evaluation technique used by several successful risk management groups. "Effective credit scoring will not only be driven by quantitative factors, such as financial ratios, but also by qualitative factors, such as the quality of management," wrote Mark Williams in *Energy & Power Risk Management* when he was running the risk management group at Citizens Power. Williams is now a risk management expert in the finance and economics department at Boston University.

At Citizens Power, an overall power marketer credit score is calculated by "aggregating quantitative and qualitative scores. We use a one-to-12 scoring range with one representing the strongest credit and 12 the weakest credit. We do not trade on an unsecured basis with power marketers scoring eight or higher," Williams wrote.

POWER MARKET RISK

In setting up the quantitative measurements, Williams looked at various ratios including "total debt/total tangible capital, return on capital, total tangible assets, earnings before interest and taxes/interest expense, current ration and cash flow/total debt. Once each ratio is calculated, the results should be evaluated against a comparative scoring key and a numeric value assigned. Upon assigning a value to all components, an overall numeric score is determined," explained Williams.

Among the qualitative measurements used by Williams are organizational structure; management reputation and control culture; and ability to deliver the commodity sold. When the qualitative measurements have been scored and a value assigned, then the qualitative measures are combined with the quantitative measures, yielding the credit score.

The Citizens Power group set up by Williams had very structured credit risk management policies in place. Relative to credit risk evaluation, the credit risk management group used three measurements to evaluate credit risk: a sixty-day accounts receivable measurement; mark to market calculations; and a Credit Value At Risk (CvaR) review, Williams said in an interview.

He encouraged a strong link with the legal department be developed to facilitate the implementation of netting agreements which can reduce the amount of overall accounts receivable exposure. If there's no netting agreement, then gross accounts receivable figures can be used as a measure.

For marking to market, Williams developed a daily price variation analysis that ensures that trader marks are consistent and the profit and loss statements are accurate. The analysis took the traders' price information and compares those numbers to the mean of three to five independent quotes. If the trader's price information varied by an established level, using a certain percentage, then the trader's price was thrown out and a mean average price was used. Williams suggested using the midpoint of the bid and ask range in order to guard against skewing the market.

CvaR gives risk managers a way to monitor whether the risk is increasing or decreasing with any given counterparty. CvaR is a window into the potential movement of mark to market should markets move adversely. When Citizens set credit limits for a counterparty, they are tied directly to internally derived ratings. These ratings were then used to set limits for sixty days accounts receivables, mark to market, and CvaR. Counterparties with lower scores were assigned lower credit limits as well as shorter duration limits. In addition, counterparty review frequency was also tied to overall credit rating. This is often overlooked, but is very important because counterparties with low scores need to be reviewed more often (that is, quarterly) than counterparties with high scores (which may be reviewed just once a year).

Increasing sophistication

As markets evolve, so does credit risk. And we've just been through a huge evolution in the last year. Boston University's Williams points out that there's been an increase in sophistication. Initially, the standard was to capture counterparty risk through a combined measurement of accounts receivable and mark-to-market exposure. The next industry advancement was the use of credit value at risk methodology and understanding the associated movement of mark-to-market. A further advancement was in understanding the exposure trading counterparties have to you as a energy company. It's a way of determining trading liquidity and estimating counterparties' willingness to extend you credit so you can successfully sell your product (electrons or gas molecules) in the market place, Williams says.

The most recent advancement has been the realization that in the energy business credit is the lifeblood of trading and as a result it is critical to keep a strong credit position. The recent failure and defaults by energy companies such as Enron, NEG and NRG drives this point home, Williams believes. If an energy company isn't investment grade (drops below BBB-), it's not going to be able to sell its product at a competitive price. "Liquidity has dried up in the market because the majority of top-10 energy trading companies have lost their investment grade standing," Williams contends. "I think management is going to think twice about leveraging balance sheets up. They also will want to have solid lines of communication with the ratings agencies. And management will need to have a better idea of how the capital markets view a change in strategy or an increase in debt that may alter the actual or perceived risk profile of the company and cause it to be downgraded."

Companies also need to look at how the debt market responds, Williams points out. For instance, companies need to be aware of the daily basis point spreads on bonds as well as credit default swap spreads. These market-based numbers are good indicators of credit risk and credit default, Williams says. Besides using third party agencies, market participants are increasingly focusing on such market-derived leading indicators to assess creditworthiness.

Chapter 9

The Fine Print: Legal and Accounting Issues

Risk management has its own specialized accounting and legal issues, and understanding their specifics and their implications is vital to the success of any risk management program. This chapter examines some of the principal concerns about risk management from the legal and accounting perspectives.

Any company starting a risk management program would do well to make certain that its staff is suitably cognizant of legal and accounting issues related to futures, derivatives and, indeed, risk management itself. While a company's legal department may be well versed in general contract law, derivatives pose special legal challenges and uncertainties. Additionally, if a company is to benefit from risk management activities, its accountants must be knowledgeable about tax rules and accounting standards that pertain to derivatives and futures.

Legal Lessons

The legal challenges aren't theory; they're fact. The wildly volatile electricity markets of the summers of

POWER MARKET RISK

1998 and 1999, as well as the events of 2001 and 2002, taught the legal community a great deal about the legal issues resulting from these spikes. A brief look at the aftermath of those events will help us understand some of the legal implications of risk management activities.

Short positions, a lack of understanding of contracts, and improper assessment of counterparty credit risk were all factors in the electricity price debacle of 1998 when an extended heat wave, the loss of key generating plants, transmission constraints, and the default of a small electric power marketer on its contract obligations converged in Midwest and hourly spot electricity prices soared to as much as $7,500 per megawatt hour. This incident was repeated in July 1999 when more unforeseen outages caused a number of utilities to impose rolling blackouts, and hourly spot market energy prices spiked to $1,000 per megawatt hour. The legal repercussions of those episodes were contract defaults, credit risk exposure and the realization that contracts were drafted poorly. Since price spikes are likely to occur in the future, it may be useful to look at how power markets could have handled those price spikes from a legal perspective.

In an article entitled, "Managing Hidden Legal Risks" which appeared in *Hart Energy Markets*, Andrea S. Kramer and Paul J. Pantano, Jr., partners at the law firm of McDermott, Will & Emery, analyzed the price spikes of 1998 and 1999 to see how contracts could have been better written to minimize the risks of those summers.

Kramer and Pantano point out: "many participants in the power trading markets do not regularly identify and analyze the risks inherent in their contracts." To avoid losses, the authors advise market participants that "they need to identify risks, understand how highly interdependent these risk are, and develop ways to measure and control these risks."

POWER MARKET RISK

The main risks in trading are market risk, credit risk, operational risk and legal risk. Kramer and Pantano say that traders watch market and credit risk closely, " but without necessarily acknowledging their interrelationship." Some consideration is also given by traders to operational risk. Kramer and Pantano contend that there are legal risks hidden in other trading risks, such as the fact that a contract may be unenforceable, and that these legal risks are often overlooked.

To lessen the likelihood of overlooking important contractual elements, Kramer and Pantano recommend the use of a master agreement, "one contract that covers all power trades entered into between the parties, regardless of which party is the buyer or seller." New to the power markets, master agreements, are now used in many derivatives trades and "provide a comprehensive structure for all power sales between two parties. The use of a master agreement could also help power traders manage their credit, operational and legal risks," according to Kramer and Pantano. Master agreements are preferable over individual contracts for each risk transaction because "separate agreements for purchases and sales do not provide the parties with the full range of protections afforded them under a master agreement. Different contracts covering purchases and sales are likely to contain different, and therefore inconsistent, terms for *force majeure*, and close-out terms for defaults or bankruptcy," Kramer and Pantano point out.

There's also a solid accounting reason to have master agreements in place. Observe Kramer and Pantano: "Without a master agreement (or at least a netting agreement) in place, a party may not be able to net profits from one contract against losses from another."

To minimize risk, Kramer and Pantano suggest that companies do the following:

POWER MARKET RISK

- Have a binding agreement;
- Make use of cross-product netting which allows the parties to offset or net the amounts due to each party on the same date. Only the party owing the larger aggregated amount makes a payment to the other party. Set the procedures for liquidated damages and the parameters of *force majeure*;
- Agree to share credit information; and
- Include representations and warranties regarding power contracts.

One of the most important representations, Kramer and Pantano say, is the assurance that "parties have legal capacity and authority to enter into power forwards, options and derivatives."

Need for Standardization

While OTC derivatives are relatively new instruments, several organizations have made strides in trying to standardize contracts, thereby lessening legal risks. Companies and individuals active in derivatives trading see a real need for standardization.

Standardization is also important in weather derivative contracts. Improved consistency and uniformity of documentation is important for the future growth of the weather market. Although the majority of derivative structures are transacted under a widely accepted International Swaps & Derivatives Association (ISDA) document, which is a standardized contract for derivatives, many possible additions and customizations must be addressed.

One of the benefits of using OTC derivatives is the possibility of customizing these instruments. However, to prevent legal ambiguities and the likelihood of litigation, there should be standardization in the contracts used for the transactions. Seeing this need for standardized contracts for derivatives as well as non-derivative based transactions, several organizations have been active in drawing up standardized contracts.

The International Swaps and Derivatives Association's Master Agreement is the standardized contract used most often for OTC derivatives. Other standardized contracts include those developed by the North American Energy Standards Board for natural gas and by the Edison Electric Institute for electricity.

The Group of Thirty strongly recommends that end-users and dealers "use one master agreement as widely as possible with each counterparty to document existing and future derivatives transactions" and that master agreements should "provide for payments netting and close-out netting, using a full two-way payments approach."

The reasons behind these recommendations are simple. If multiple master agreements are used, The Group warns, there's a risk that the parties will pick and choose among the master agreements, choosing only those which favor the respective party, which could cause havoc. A single master agreement can be used to document many derivatives transactions. "A single master agreement that documents [all] transactions between two parties creates the greatest legal certainty that credit exposure will be netted, thereby ensuring that a payment due to a party will be paid. If full two way netting isn't used, a party that defaults might not receive payment even if payment is due. The practices of using separate agreements for each transaction between two parties, or standard terms that do not constitute a master agreement, are not good practices and should be discontinued."

The Group further comments that the use of full two-

POWER MARKET RISK

way payments is the preferred approach under master agreements because they discourage default. Under this system, "the net amount calculated through the netting provisions in a bilateral master agreement is due regardless of whether it is to, or from, the defaulting party." If a limited two-way payment system is used, the defaulting party isn't entitled to receive any payment, "even if the net amount is in its favor." While limited two-way payment systems discourage default, The Group contends, "The benefits created by increasing the certainty about the value of a net position under full two-way payments outweigh any possible benefits under limited two-way payments." In other words, legal wrangling is minimized.

International Swaps and Derivatives Association

The International Swaps and Derivatives Association (ISDA) has developed a master agreement that has established international contractual standards governing privately negotiated derivatives transactions. ISDA is a global trade association that represents leading participants in the derivatives market and currently has 575 members worldwide.

ISDA was established to:
- Promote practices conducive to the efficient conduct of the business of its member in swaps and other derivatives, including the development and maintenance of standard documentation for derivatives, and to foster high standards of commercial honor and business conduct among its members;
- Create a forum for the discussion of issues of relevance to participants in derivatives transactions and to cooperate with other organizations on issues of mutual concern in order to promote com-

mon interests;
- Advance international public understanding of derivatives;
- Inform its members of legislative and administrative developments affecting participants in derivatives transactions; to provide a forum for its members to examine and review such developments; and to represent effectively the common interests of its members before legislative and administrative bodies and international quasi-public institutes, boards and other bodies; and
- Encourage the development and maintenance of an efficient and productive market for derivatives through action in furtherance of the foregoing purpose.

ISDA also works "to develop and improve risk management practices and policies among its members and among derivative industry participants in general."

ISDA's Master Agreement "has established international contractual standards governing privately negotiated derivatives transactions that reduce legal uncertainty and allow for reduction of credit risk through netting of contractual obligations." As the business has developed and grown, ISDA has expanded and updated the Master Agreement and its supporting documents, and the process is ongoing.

The 1992 ISDA Master Agreement comes in two forms: one for local currency, single jurisdictions and one for multi-currency, cross border transactions. Attorney Kramer says her law firm typically uses the multi-currency, cross border form of the agreement since the parties know they can use that for all counterparties.

The Master Agreement document sets out an agreement between two counterparties in clear language. The

POWER MARKET RISK

document is a complete contract consisting of sections on interpretation, obligations, representations, events of default and termination events, early termination, transfer, expenses, notices, governing law and jurisdiction, and definitions. At the very least, the contract can be used as a starting point for derivative contract negotiations, suggests attorney Kramer.

Companion booklets to the Master Agreement are the 2000 ISDA Definitions and the 2000 Supplement to the 1993 ISDA Commodity Derivatives Definitions. Copies of the Master Agreement and the definition booklets can be purchased from ISDA. See the resources section for contact information. These definitions are intended for use with the Master Agreement and are "designed for use by participants in the markets for commodity derivative transactions to document cash-settled commodity swaps, options, caps, collars, floors and swaptions or such other cash-settled commodity derivative transactions as the parties desire." The definitions give the reference for the price or index being used and details about the price or index.

Other Types of Standardized Contracts

Three other organizations, the North American Energy Standards Board (NAESB) and the Edison Electric Institute, have developed standardized contracts for natural gas and electricity, respectively. The Weather Risk Management Association (WRMA) has developed confirmations and contracts for weather derivatives.

NAESB

Created in January 2002, NAESB is a non-profit association to develop standards for the retail and wholesale natural gas and electricity industries. NAESB has absorbed the Gas Industry Standards Board (GISB). In 1996, GISB released its model short-term gas sales and purchase contract. "The contract is designed to make natural gas easier to buy and sell by standardizing language and business provisions," the Board says. The model contract is intended for interruptible or firm transactions of one month or less and contains three parts: the base contract, a general terms and conditions section, and a transaction confirmation and is designed to be adaptable to changing industry conditions and provisions.

Edison Electric Institute

The Edison Electric Institute, an association of U.S. investor-owned electric utilities and industry affiliates, had developed a standardized wholesale electric trading contract, which has become quite popular.

"The ultimate purpose of this effort is to increase the liquidity of electric markets by establishing standard contract terms that allow traders to focus on the basic negotiable elements of a given transaction (e.g., price and quantity)." The contract is intended to facilitate physical delivery of electricity.

Increased competition in power markets has pointed up the need for an electricity agreement that contains standard contract language and incorporates and defines trading practices and terms. Many documents are now used for wholesale transactions including cost-based tariffs, market-based rate tariffs and service agreements, unilateral and bilateral contracts and pool-enabled transactions, says EEI. Therefore, standardization of contracts would be exceedingly useful in the electric power markets

The Standardized Master Power Contract is designed to contain the core terms and conditions needed to establish trading relationships between counterparties. The

POWER MARKET RISK

contract establishes standardized terms "essential for all transactions, enabling traders to focus on product, price quantity, duration, and delivery," says EEI. The electricity master agreement spells out the obligations of the parties who sell and buy these products, addresses credit risk and other legal considerations. The benefits of the Master Contract include: streamlines establishing a trading relationship; provides real time credit provisions; standardized product definitions; and focuses traders on the transaction's basic negotiable elements such as price, quantity, location, and duration.

In October 2002, EEI unveiled a new Master Netting Agreement. This is a standardized master contract that will help mitigate credit risk for energy traders. The new contract will allow trading counterparties to net their collateral requirements when making wholesale power trades, and it will offset positive balances of one transaction with negative balances of another, says EEI. Netting helps minimize counterparty exposure and capital required to trade.

"This new Master Netting Agreement is an essential tool that will help stem the tide of shrinking liquidity and lack of access to capital markets that our industry now faces," says Thomas R. Kuhn, president of EEI. "We believe the new contract should help ease the current financial crisis that has been threatening the ability of electric power companies to provide a reliable supply of energy at affordable prices."

Standardized contracts and master agreements are extremely effective in developing workable contractual obligations. Nevertheless, these agreements won't eliminate risk completely – even with contracts in place, a certain amount of legal risk remains.

Weather Risk Management Association

With weather becoming a component of many utilities' risk management programs and with more weather derivatives being traded, the Weather Risk Management Association (WRMA) was formed in June of 1999. Based in Washington, DC, the association has a diverse membership of trading companies, utilities, and other firms interested in weather derivatives.

The weather market has grown markedly over the last few years. WRMA's second annual study of the marketplace, conducted jointly with PricewaterhouseCoopers, the number of contracts transacted in the weather market grew by 43 percent for the 2001-2002 period with 3,937 weather transactions completed for a total notional value of over $4.3 billion dollars. According to the first annual survey, there were 2,759 transactions done worth a total notional value of over $2.5 billion.

To bring standardization to the weather market, WRMA has developed standardized confirmations and contracts for average temperature, cooling and heating degree-days, and precipitation derivatives. The confirmations and contracts are now available online on the association's website (www.wrma.org).

Defining Legal Risk

"Legal risk is the risk of loss because a contract cannot be enforced. This includes risks arising from insufficient documentation, insufficient capacity or authority of a counterparty, uncertain legality, and unenforceability in bankruptcy or insolvency, "according to The Group of Thirty.

Financial institutions encountered these legal risks in the conduct of their traditional business. But "the risks come in new forms with derivatives," remarks The Group.

According to the Group of Thirty, better understanding of derivatives economics and the nature of derivatives transactions has provided answers to questions about derivatives such as, what is a derivative and how does it fit into a given legislative or regulatory scheme. Standard documentation has helped ease legal concerns in some areas, but legal issues about enforceability still exist.

Enforceability risk results from the possibility that a derivatives contract "might be found to be unenforceable," the Group says. "This might result from one's counterparty being legally incapable of entering into the contract or from an entire class of contracts being declared illegal or unenforceable" or for a number of other reasons.

There are also questions about the enforceability of close-out netting provisions in master agreements.

Says The Group: "There is the possibility that a bankruptcy trustee or liquidator could attempt to cherry-pick among the swaps documented under a master agreement, enforcing only those that have positive value to the party in bankruptcy or liquidation." Further, "there are some obstacles to immediate termination of swaps when a default takes place."

Contract enforceability is the number one legal risk. But there are other legal risks that need to be addressed. In an article entitled "Derivatives and Legal Risks: Practical Protective Steps: published in *The Review of Banking & Financial Services,* Andrea S. Kramer, a partner with McDermott, Will & Emery, and Alton B. Harris, a partner with Coffield, Ungaretti & Harris, say that there are other legal risks to be considered, including protections in the event of counterparty insolvency; adequacy of credit arrangement; documentation pitfalls; dispute resolution mechanism; and suitability representations and disclaimers.

"The risk of insolvency or bankruptcy of one of the parties to a derivatives transaction is a major concern," comment Kramer and Harris. For the purposes of the U. S. Bankruptcy Code, swaps and other derivatives are considered executory contracts. "This means that without special [Bankruptcy] Code provisions, upon the filing of a petition in bankruptcy, the non-bankrupt party cannot terminate the agreement." Therefore, the non-bankrupt party must wait for the bankruptcy trustee or DIP to decide if the agreement will be rejected. "During this waiting period, the non-bankrupt party would not know whether to replace its derivatives position. If the non-bankrupt party replaces the swap, it could be bound by two swaps if the trustee ultimately assumes the swap. On the other hand, if the non-bankrupt party does not replace the swap, it could be exposed to additional loss (as a result of possible adverse movements) if the trustee ultimately rejected the swap," say Kramer and Harris.

However, under amendments to the Bankruptcy Code, certain rights have been given to a non-bankrupt counterparty that will help the counterparty's situation. According to Kramer and Harris, those rights under the amendments are that the non-bankrupt party can set off any mutual obligation regarding the swap and use the debtor's cash securities or other property to satisfy payments due from the debtor.

Any rights in the agreement to terminate the swap on a bankruptcy termination are respected and that provisions in the master agreement for close-out netting are enforceable upon termination of the swap. "If the non-bankrupt party has more than one swap with the debtor under a master agreement, all agreements are taken together and viewed as a single swap, thereby preventing a trustee from cherry-picking individual transactions."

Credit Arrangements

To avoid the risk of a counterparty becoming insolvent, a thorough counterparty credit analysis must be performed before a derivative transaction takes place. To address credit concerns, counterparties often rely on third party guarantees, letters of credit or collateral agreements.

However, literal readings of the Bankruptcy Code could present problems for collateral agreements unless those agreements are handled correctly. That is, a literal reading of the law would exclude collateral agreements from the preferential transfer provisions of the law. To avoid that outcome, Kramer and Harris suggest that "collateral and security agreements should be incorporated by reference directly into, and made a part of, the master agreement."

Documentation Pitfalls

"Proper documentation is critical to assure that derivative transactions are enforceable as negotiated by the parties," Kramer and Harris say. More and more contracts are being done on a standardized basis, with ISDA master agreements being used most frequently.

"A key point to remember is that standardized documents really just serve as a starting point. As a result, schedules to master agreements are often extensively and painstakingly negotiated to reflect actual business and legal terms," remark Kramer and Harris. Further, the attorneys say: "proper documentation must address a wide range of provisions, including, for example, netting provisions (on a transaction-by-transaction basis or across product types); credit support (typically through security agreements, guarantees, or letters of credit); representations and warranties (as to authority, suitability, tax withholding, and the provision of necessary tax documents); covenants; and events of default."

There can be pitfalls, however, even with documentation. Kramer and Harris say provisions that must be looked at closely include those for limited two-way payments (full two-way payments are preferred); market quotation or loss; cross default; and set off rights.

Under limited two-way payments, the non-defaulting party "can walk away from its obligations if the counterparty defaults and never pays anything." In full two-way payments, " the settlement amounts and unpaid amounts are aggregated. The party with a net profit is paid by the party with a net loss." So if the defaulting party is the one with the net profit, it would still receive payment.

Parties may use either market quotation or loss as a way to calculate the settlements amount. In the market quotation method, the nondefaulting party determines the settlement amount based on quotes from market makers. The loss method allows the nondefaulting party to determine its total losses and costs in regards to the agreements. Any amounts that are unpaid are included in a party's loss.

Cross-default provisions are a way of saying that default occurs if "there is a default by a 'specified entity' relating to a 'specified indebtedness' in an amount that exceeds the 'threshold amount.'" Specified entities are usually third-party affiliates. Therefore, problems with counterparty's affiliate could prevent the counterparty from fulfilling an obligation.

Provisions for acceptable set-off rights should be included in an agreement. Without a set-off clause, the nondefaulting party "may be required to make payment to the defaulting party upon termination and, at the same time, not have any realistic expectation of receiving payments owed to it by the defaulting party and its affiliates."

Dispute Resolution Mechanism

Many swap counterparties have included waivers of jury trials in the schedules to master agreements in the event of a dispute, according to Kramer and Harris. Some parties may not wish to go to the time and expense involved in jury trials.

Some counterparties prefer to resolve their disputes under alternative dispute resolution provisions. Kramer and Harris explain that ADR provisions can stipulate negotiation between the parties, non-binding mediation, and binding arbitration.

Suitability Representations and Valuation Disclaimers

As litigation over derivatives losses increases, dealers are becoming more sensitive to counterparty claims that dealers are responsible for the counterparty losses. Kramer and Harris explain, "in early 1995, ISDA released standard representations of non-reliance that can be included in schedules to, or amendments of, ISDA master agreements" to clarify dealers' limited responsibility for losses.

Among the non-reliance representations that can used are that "the parties are 'not relying' on the advice of the counterparty; each counterparty "has consulted with its own advisors as to the 'suitability' of any transactions" and "each party has 'a full understanding of all of the terms, conditions and risks (economic and otherwise)' of the agreement and transactions and is 'capable' and

POWER MARKET RISK

'willing' to 'assume (financially and otherwise)' these risks."

Handling the Future

As the derivatives market grows, new types of transactions will be developed and new technologies will be created to confirm the deals, points out The Group of Thirty. Since these developments might not fall clearly under existing laws, The Group of Thirty calls upon dealers and end-users to "work together to evaluate developments in light of existing laws to assess what legal issues may arise. They should take the initiative to ensure that risks arising from these developments can be properly handled through analysis, market practices, documentation, and, when necessary, legislation."

A Few Words on Regulatory Oversight

Since OTC derivatives began to be used on a regular basis, there has been much discussion about whether there should be more regulatory oversight over these currently unregulated instruments. When major events have occurred involving derivatives—such as the Orange County, California debacle where the county government was forced to declare bankruptcy because of massive losses from leveraged investments in financial derivatives or the downfall of Barings where inadequately controlled speculation in Japanese stock index futures by a trader caused the collapse of Britain's oldest merchant bank—there has been a clamor for more regulation of the derivatives market.

The recent energy scandals involving Enron and the manipulation of the California energy markets also have

POWER MARKET RISK

spurred legislators to propose more regulation for the energy markets. But all the legislation in the world can't make up for lax oversight on the part of companies using financial instruments to hedge risk. All financial instruments used in managing risk must be watched on a daily basis. There is no excuse for allowing derivatives or any other financial instrument to be used without proper oversight.

The Group of Thirty believed that no "fundamental changes in the current regulatory framework, such as separate regulation of this [derivatives market] activity, are needed. Separate regulation of global derivatives would be at cross-purposes with the existing framework of supervisions, with its focus on the common risks contained in derivatives and traditional instruments. There is also a danger in imposing regulatory formulas that inhibit new product innovation or discourage firms from developing the individualized, robust risk management systems on which they should rely."

Recommendations were presented about altering the Commodity Exchange Act to facilitate use of OTC derivatives. The President's Working Group on Financial Markets released its report on over-the-counter derivatives in November 1999. The President's Working Group, headed by Lawrence Summers, Secretary of the Treasury; Alan Greenspan, Chairman of the Federal Reserve; Arthur Levitt, Chairman of the Securities and Exchange Commission; and William Rainer, Chairman of the Commodity Futures Trading Commission, made a number of recommendations for changes to the Commodity Exchange Act (CEA).

These changes are designed to make it easier for derivatives to be traded. Among the report's recommendations are creating a exclusion from the CEA for swaps agreements that are bilateral agreements between eligible

POWER MARKET RISK

parties on a principal to principal basis. This recommendation provides greater legal certainty and removes doubts about enforceability, making the U.S. a more attractive derivatives market. Another recommendation advises creating an exclusion from the CEA for electronic trading systems that limit participation to sophisticated parties trading for their own accounts. The Treasury says this recommendation promotes innovation, competition, efficiency, liquidity and transparency and encourages the development of electronic trading systems. A third recommendation advocates removing legal impediments to the development of clearing systems, similar to those that exist for futures exchanges, for OTC derivatives which the U.S. Treasury says would reduce system risk by encouraging appropriately regulated clearing for OTC derivatives. Clearing generally refers to the registration and settlement of a trade and includes provisions for margin requirement and performance guarantee.

In December 2000, the Commodity Futures Modernization Act of 2000 (CFMA) was signed into law. This sweeping revision of the Commodity Exchange Act basically adopted the changes recommended by The President's Working Group. One of the key parts of the legislation is that it virtually eliminates the chance that an OTC derivative contract between "eligible contract participants" could be voided as an illegal off-exchange futures contract, says the Association for Financial Professionals.

Accounting Issues

Risk management also needs to consider taxation and accounting issues, especially those concerning derivatives. As an overview of the accounting issues involved in derivatives, here are The Group of Thirty's accounting recommendations:

- Dealers should account for derivatives transactions by marking them to market, taking changes in value to income each period.
- End-users should account for derivatives used to manage risks so as to achieve a consistency of income recognition treatment between those instruments and the risks being managed. Thus, if the risk being managed is accounted for at cost (or, in the case of anticipatory hedge, not yet recognized), changes in the value of a qualified risk management instrument should be deferred until a gain or loss is recognized on the risk being managed. Or, if the risk being managed is marked to market with changes in value being taken to income, a qualifying risk management instrument should be treated in a comparable fashion.
- End-users should account for derivatives not qualifying for risk management treatment on a mark-to-market basis.
- Amounts due to and from counterparties should only be offset when there is a legal right to set off or when enforceable netting arrangements are in place.
- The Group says that 'where local regulations prevent adoption of these practices, disclosure along these lines in nevertheless recommended."

Adopting these suggestions would mean that accounting for derivatives would be more accurate and that better accounting practices will assist in better risk management.

In response to The Group's recommendations, a few new rules and regulations concerning how to handle derivatives transactions have been promulgated over the last few years. The main accounting rule that will affect derivatives in the U.S. is the Financial Accounting Standards Board's Statement No. 133, commonly known as Statement No.133.

Statement No.133 went into effect with fiscal years beginning after June 15, 2000. Originally slated to go into effect a year earlier, concerns about companies' abilities to modify information systems and educate managers caused FASB to delay implementation of Standard 133. The effective date change was noted in the FASB Statement of Accounting Standards No. 137.

One of the most significant accounting and reporting changes for some companies was the fair value aspect of accounting for derivative instruments. Statement No.133 establishes accounting and reporting standards for derivative instruments, including those embedded in other contracts and used for hedging activities. The standard calls for a company to recognize all derivatives as either assets or liabilities in its financial statement and to measure those instruments at fair market value The accounting board defines a derivative as "(a) a hedge of the exposure to changes in the fair value of recognized assets or liability or an unrecognized firm commitment, (b) a hedge of the exposure to variable cash slows of a forecasted transaction, or (c) a hedge of the foreign currency exposures of a net investment in a foreign operation, an unrecognized firm commitment, an available-for-sale security, or a foreign-currency-denominated forecasted transaction."

According to FASB, how changes in the value of a derivative are accounted for depends on the intended use of the derivative and the resulting designation. Says the accounting board:

POWER MARKET RISK

- For a derivative designated as hedging the exposure to changes in the fair value of a recognized assets or liability or a firm commitment (referred to as a *fair value hedge*), the gain or loss is recognized in earnings in the period of change together with the offsetting loss or gain on the hedged item attributable to the risk being hedged. The effect of that accounting is to reflect in earnings the extent to which the hedge is not effective in achieving offsetting change in fair value.
- For a derivative designated as hedging the exposure to variable cash flows of a forecasted transaction (referred to as a *cash flow hedge*), the effective portion of the derivative's gain or loss is initially reported as a component of other comprehensive income (outside earnings) and subsequently reclassified into earnings when the forecasted transaction affects earnings. The ineffective portion of the gain or loss is reported in earnings immediately.
- For a derivative designated as hedging the *foreign currency exposure* of a net investment in a foreign operation, the gain or loss is reported in other comprehensive income (outside earnings) as part of the cumulative translation adjustment. The accounting for a fair value hedge described above applies to a derivative designated as a hedge of the foreign currency exposure of an unrecognized firm commitment or an available-for-sale security. Similarly, the accounting for a cash flow hedge described above applies to a derivative designated as a hedge of the foreign currency exposure of a foreign-currency-denominated forecasted transaction.

POWER MARKET RISK

- For a derivative not designated as a hedging instrument, the gain or loss is recognized in earnings in the period of change.

Statement No.133 requires that an entity that elects to apply hedge accounting must first establish the method it will use for measuring both the effectiveness and the ineffectiveness of the hedging derivative. Both methods must be consistent with the entity's approach to managing risk.

Statement No.133 conforms to the very principles of risk management. The accounting must be consistent with a company's risk management strategy, and the hedge accounting must be established at the beginning of the process, not later.

The standard also states that energy trading contracts that can effectively be net settled [that is netted out] will generally be considered to be derivatives and will fall under Statement No.133 jurisdiction. However, some transportation and other energy-related contracts may represent lease transactions which fall outside Statement No.133 authority.

Interestingly, exchange traded weather contracts, like the Chicago Mercantile Exchange futures contracts, do fall under jurisdiction of Statement No.133. However, weather contracts that aren't traded on an exchange aren't subject to Statement No.133 "if the settlement is based on a climatic or geological variable or some other physical variable." FASB's Emerging Issues Task Force released an abstract entitled *Accounting for Weather Derivatives, Issue No. 99-2* in July 1999, which reviews weather derivatives -- differentiating trading from non-trading contracts -- and the accounting methods to be used.

POWER MARKET RISK

In June 2000, FASB issued an amendment to Statement 133, known as Statement 138. According to FASB, the Statement 138 amends Statement 133 such that:

- The normal purchases and normal sales exception is expanded.
- The specific risks that can be identified as the hedged risk are redefined so that in a hedge of interest rate risk the risk of changes in a benchmark interest rate would be the hedged risk.
- Recognized foreign-currency-denominated assets and liabilities may be the hedged item in fair value hedges or cash flow hedges.
- Intercompany derivatives may be designated as the hedging instruments in cash flow hedges of foreign currency risk in the consolidated financial statements even if those intercompany derivatives are offset by unrelated third-party contracts on a net basis.

As you can see, FASB Statements are works in progress. Likely, there will be additional Amendments to Statement 133 as the Board continues to fine-tune the standard.

If you study these various documents and contracts, you'll have a good understanding of legal and accounting issues. But, you'll have to remember that problems like credit risk (see Chapter 8) can throw your best-laid plans into disarray.

Chapter 10:

Knowledge, Not Data: Using CI To Avoid Pitfalls

"How did we let that happen?" How often have you heard business people say that? It's often paired with: "Well, no one would have guessed..."

But often, the seeds of disasters and marketplace reverses are quite clear, in hindsight. The trouble is, what use is hindsight? What you need is a way of foreseeing and predicting problems, so you can avoid them. That knowledge can be obtained by a careful application of the art of competitive intelligence.

So, what is 'competitive intelligence'? As practiced by corporations today, it is the gathering and analysis of information on what is happening in their marketplace, what their competitors are doing, and what rival companies are thinking. Typically, the CI function is used to support the efforts of strategists at senior management level, to keep marketing departments aware of what is really going on outside their own wishful scenarios, and to alert research groups to technological threats. But a corporation can use CI in almost any context. We recommend that it become an integral part of your thinking about Risk Management.

POWER MARKET RISK

Why would a utility, for example, care about what competitors do? Once upon a time, in the days of strong regulation, this would have been a perfectly apt response. But in deregulated markets, an efficient CI effort is *de rigueur*. To traders, suppliers and customers, it is just as vital.

It's quite easy for senior management to respond to the CI idea with the typical knee-jerk reactions that we're so familiar with: "We're drowning in data!"; "Not another report to read!"; "There's not enough time in the day," and the like. But the plain fact is, you have to make time. If you don't have a bird's eye view of the marketplace and your competitors', suppliers' and customers' activities and intentions, you're just flying blind. Running your business on a case-by-case, crisis management basis is a recipe for disaster.

A CI function is another expense. But at the same time *it's just another expense or cost of doing business*. It's as vital as any other function in a corporation's business toolkit. Without it, you're winging it. With it, you make informed decisions.

CI In An Power Industry Context

Obviously, the information needs of a power industry company are different from those of say, a food industry conglomerate, a pharmaceutical company, or a consumer goods manufacturer. You should aim to tailor your CI operation to fit the needs of a selection of interested parties within the corporation. They are:
- The Board of Directors
- The CEO and Management Committee
- The Risk Management group
- Marketing/Sales
- Finance

Before you even start setting up – or modifying – a CI Group to meet the challenges of tomorrow's turbulent markets, you need to get 'buy in' from all of these groups. You – the CEO, CRO or whoever is pioneering this idea – will have to sell them on the vital nature of the concept, and cite examples of how this works for other corporations. We'll offer some hints on that at the end of the chapter.

'Buy in' is vital.

The key questions they will ask, after 'what will this add to my budget?' will be:

- What is the **scope** of the department's responsibility?
- How will it operate and **report** to the corporate structure?
- How widely should its findings be **disseminated**?
- Can we make **'requests'** or add to its list of monitorings?
- Is this going to be fully **integrated** with our IT or knowledge management?

To some extent, these questions should define their own answers.

On **scope**, we'd suggest that the CI group be allowed, or be instructed, to monitor activity and intentions of any company doing a significant amount of business with your corporation – buying or selling. The threshold will depend on your taste for naked risk. Perhaps $1 million plus? Perhaps $5MM? Perhaps $10MM? We wouldn't suggest setting it any higher.

On **responsibility**, there is an excellent argument for having this group report to both the CEO and the CRO.

Practices vary, and in many companies outside the power business, marketing tends to pay for CI, out of its deep pockets, and has a lot to say about how it is practiced. But since you're concerned about *strategy* and *risk,* it would appear wise to let those with the greatest responsibility have the car keys.

On **dissemination:** this is a tricky point. You clearly want to avoid having sensitive – maybe potentially damaging – business information in too many hands. It's not supposed to be an in-house newsletter for everyone wearing a business suit! But equally, you need to make sure that *involved* parties aren't kept in the dark about CI discoveries and warnings. We'll discuss *how* to distribute this information below.

On **requests:** it's perfectly proper to ask the CI department to look into a specific problem that arises, concerning one of the interested departments. What you want to avoid, however, is having it turn into a general-purpose, odd-job department that gets saddled with any 'search' job that comes along. It's not an extension of the library!

On **integration:** How much you choose integrate this with Knowledge Management or IT depends entirely on your corporate culture. If you are avid users of a confidential Intranet, or a file-sharing software package like Lotus Notes, you might want to release CI data there. If there is a separate executive intelligence report made available on- or offline, it might go there. Our sense is that the wave of the future is in electronic delivery and constant online access, and that you'll find this more effective in the long run.

Setting goals

What sort of 'information' are you going to try to capture? How will it supplement what busy executives do in

POWER MARKET RISK

the course of their normal working day? Clearly, you need to set some parameters if this isn't going to mushroom into some unmanageable mess. Here are some basic decisions to take:

- Identify your principal competitors *now,* and try to identify likely *future* competitors
- Identify your current suppliers and customers, weeding out those below a threshold size, *if* they do not have some strategically important responsibility that you cannot possibly afford to have compromised. This might be something as small as a printshop you use for marketing materials, for example. Or maybe a maintenance contract on electricity meters.
- Have a clear idea *what risk means* in the context of these players. Is it their bankruptcy? Is it a business scenario where they cease to be suppliers, or are acquired by a competitor? Use some creative, lateral thinking to define what kinds of threats are realistic, and to derive some that are less likely but still liable to cause business disruptions
- What drives your business? If you're a utility, it may well be down to (i) upsets in consumer demand (ii) security of supply and (iii) maintenance of 'wires and poles.' Use this information to refine your idea of items at risk.
- In the end, the CRO's staff will make the risk assessments. But you need to be sure that the CI staff share a view of what is a real risk (>30% probability) and marginal risk (say, < 5%), so they don't plague the CRO with 'penny ante problems.'
- Having defined the players and topics, map

POWER MARKET RISK

out where this information is most likely to be found, or how it can be monitored on an ongoing basis. That part of the task is best done by the CI professionals you hire, but you should expect them to want to hear viewpoints and ideas from all interested parties.

- A *lot* of what the CI people will monitor will be publicly available information. They'll be reading annual reports, 10Ks and 10Qs, other SEC documents, FERC reports; studying the general press and the specialized trade press; obtaining conference papers or presentations by the target companies; monitoring web pages; and setting up search profiles to look for signs of competitor activity that crop up on the Internet. If you're a company with a technology bent, you may find they'll need to study patent filings by competitors.

Who Contributes?

It's amazing, but true.

You *already know* far more than you think you do about what's happening in the market, or what your competitors, suppliers and customers are up to. Unless your staff is braindead, they're picking up important information by the hour.

Think about it: you have salespeople, there are customers calling in to help desks; while executives often make direct contacts with competitors at conferences. Finance types get to know a lot about the business practices of suppliers and customers, some of it highly valuable.

What you need to do is to harness the power of all this knowledge. And to do it, it needs to be made clear by the CEO and CRO that they *value input.* They need to make this clear by word and deed, and not rebuff tipsters with the phrase: 'Oh sure, we know all about that. We're on top of it. Back to your cubicle!" Like so much in business, it's a corporate cultural issue. You need to encourage communication of ideas and intelligence from below.

What's The Product?

No, it's not about what your company sells. What's the CI product? How will this mountain of information get refined from ore into gold? How do you prevent a blizzard of paper or e-mail that overwhelms the CI clients?

To a great extent, this depends on the preferences of the stakeholders. The board of directors, for example, might like a monthly or quarterly memo of a few pages to consider in advance of a meeting. The CEO, perhaps, would ask for a weekly memo, prepared for his consideration. The CRO and staff might require a daily digest, and an e-mail alert about some particularly odd development.

The key point is to *stick to the point*. Let these reports focus on the major risks, or developing ones, rather than summarize every single discovery. It's up to the business acumen and common sense of the CI staff to accommodate their stakeholders needs, and they should all confer on this at regular intervals to adjust the process.

A key part of CI is *tuning*. This will probably be done informally during the course of a day, but the CI department should have a weekly meeting to review what it has found, and what it proposes to pass on. The CRO should send a representative to this meeting, and should attend any other meeting that discusses broad CI policy.

Knowledge Management and CI

A word on integration. We've already suggested that the wave of the future is towards widespread use of Knowledge Management systems within corporations. They're already commonplace in Fortune 500 companies, helping tame the flood of data from E-commerce, or enabling pharmaceutical companies to keep tags on data-intensive tasks like genomic-related research. It's an oversimplification, but they do this by careful indexing of all documents in a company's databases, using XML to 'tag' information rather than the familiar HTML encoding language that drives the Internet today. By building an 'ontology' – think of it as a family tree – of documents, you can speed up searches of related topics.

Clearly, this has strong implications for CI, especially the handling of fragments of information that may exist in documents of different forms in-house. Whether you're looking at sales reports in Word, Excel spreadsheets, PDF documents, Powerpoint presentations, or data in some half-remembered file format from the 1980s, they can all be accessed just as easily using KM systems, after the XML is added.

We'd encourage you to investigate this possibility quite seriously, if you have not done so already.

Build it or buy it?

So, do you set up a CI department of your own, or do you buy services from a professional CI company outside? This has been a dilemma for some, although increasingly, companies are bringing this vital function in-house.

The arguments in favor are pretty persuasive:
- You have direct control of what is researched, and

why
- You have the security of knowing that no one outside the metaphorical 'four walls' of the corporation need be aware of your strategic concerns and risk exposure profile
- You're not doing business with someone who might have worked for a competitor
- The ethics and practices of an in-house CI operation are your own

The argument *against* is best summarized that 'some people know things you don't know,' and 'a fresh eye often spots things you have become too close to.'

There are many professional CI companies who'll work on a 'one-time' or retainer basis for corporate clients. Typically, companies employ these organizations when they feel extreme doubt about some particular problem, and want a dispassionate opinion from someone who will not be pressured to reach any particular conclusion. Someone who'll dare to say something contrarian, or not be bothered if some internal interest group is offended by the findings.

It's sad but true that CI has acquired something of a 'dodgy' reputation in recent years. There have been cases of practitioners pretending to be graduate students to tap the brains of competitors, or even of 'dumpster divers' retrieving unshredded corporate documents from the trash bins of corporations.

Have no part of this: it's unethical and illegal.

And it may backfire on you in other ways. We know of several companies that use IP address recognition to 'steer' hits on their websites to bogus sites filled with disinformation and shorn of useful intelligence. How would you be sure those 'dumpster files' weren't clever fakes?

POWER MARKET RISK

A Case Study: 'The Oil Company Threat'

An example of how an outside CI company can be helpful. A large utility once retained The Thinking Companies to assess a possible competitive threat that had divided opinions among its senior executives. We won't tell you the answer, but we'll explain the question and the methodology as a good example of what CI can do.

We were asked: "*Is there a possibility of major oil companies entering the consumer electricity market after deregulation? And if so, is anyone making plans?*"

Think it through, and you'll see the logic: Major refiners and gasoline companies have all the 'kit' – credit cards, huge databases of consumers, the 'back rooms' to process sales in quite small denominations – gas tank-sized – and a great marketing opportunity in every envelope they mail with a monthly bill. With dereg, they can buy electricity easily – their own finances are strong – and send it down 'your' wires to 'your' customers. Maybe even shaving prices to buy market share at first.

We used two research methods. One 'anyone' could do; another only 'an outsider' could do.

On the 'anyone' front, we searched high and low for indications in FERC documents, company reports, and state agency records. And found a surprisingly large amount of evidence that the client hadn't seen.

On the 'outsider' front, we directly interviewed executives at all the major oil companies – yes, it's like pulling teeth! – to gauge their attitudes to entering the retail electricity markets, and to follow up on the few actual test marketing cases that were underway, albeit very quietly, in some states.

Result: a happy client. The threat, as perceived, wasn't quite ready to materialize. Of course, in a few years ...

Chapter 11

Uneven Playing Fields: Dealing with Rigged Markets

There's no better way to start this chapter than by quoting verbatim from our earlier book:

> **"A Lesson From The Oil Market**
>
> Perhaps it might be instructive to see how other parts of the energy market have dealt with dramatic changes in market structure and embraced risk management ideas. The experience of the oil market, while not completely analogous to the utility market, may shed some light on how companies made the transition from a regulated to an unregulated marketplace and used risk management techniques to minimize the volatility of the new market structure.
>
> I reported on oil markets for fourteen years at McGraw-Hill's *Platt's* [writes Shirley Savage]. My days of covering the oil business started in 1984 when the futures market for crude oil was fairly new as was the spot or cash market. A spot market is simply the one time purchase of a commodity. The buyer and seller agree on the price to be paid. In the early 1980s, many of the experienced crude oil traders - and products

traders - disliked the New York Mercantile Exchange futures market. They called them 'Atari barrels,' named after a computer favored by games players. Oil traders were often disparaging about the NYMEX and suggested, rather rudely, that a dentist trading speculatively could sway futures prices. The oil traders prided themselves on remaining in a supply and demand driven market that wasn't influenced by fluctuations of the futures price. And certainly, movements on the futures market were far from radical on a day-to-day basis. In the refined products markets, it was a momentous event when futures moved 1¢ per gallon during the day.

But the separation between the church of fundamental cash market trade and the state called NYMEX didn't last long. It was the market crash of 1985-1986, and the resulting volatile market, that made some 'old school' oil traders sit up and take notice. There was one day during the tumult that traders sat back in disbelief at the volatility rocking the market - instead of a 1¢ move in futures product prices, the futures price swung 8¢ in a single trading day. That was when traders knew volatility was here to stay. Volatility has been part of the oil market ever since.

Until the oil crisis of 1985-1986, some oil traders hadn't seriously considered using futures as a way to hedge risk. Granted, some oil companies had been using oil futures to hedge right from the start of the NYMEX contracts. But others were slower to make the move. By the early 1990s, however, the idea of mitigating risk by using the futures market had become widely accepted in the oil business. Further, companies were seeking other ways to mitigate risk and turned increasingly to OTC instruments. Hedging became an essential part of trading.

There is one downside to the enthusiastic embrace of hedging in the oil markets, however: as more companies struck derivatives deals, the derivatives began to drive the spot market trades. That is, cash market deals were done in order to protect a company's hedge or derivative position. It made for some bizarre cash market deals. For instance, a seller of crude oil might take out a lower bid, ignoring a higher bid that was visible in the marketplace, because the lower bid benefited the seller's derivative position. The seller might insist that the lower bid was where the market was in order to save face and blow smoke over the true reason for the deal. But the real spot market likely was higher than the level where the deal was done. Obviously this kind of behavior can't happen on a regulated futures exchange.

While I'm not to suggesting that the power markets will follow the exact same scenario, it would be wise to watch cautiously how the markets evolve because traders will utilize market advantages in order to make a profit. And developments in trading techniques and strategies will affect the tools used by a company to manage its risk. By being aware of these trading changes, a company can adjust its risk management program to keep its revenue secure."

Two years later, would we say anything different? Well, yes. We'd eliminate some of the conditionality! We might even be tempted to say *"we told you so, kinda ..."*

But rather than experiencing such simple 'rigging' develop, the market has seen many examples of blatant manipulation in the meantime.

It's clear that the idea of markets as a 'level playing

field' is open to question.

Fair or 'perfect' markets were always an ideal, theoretical concept. Because they were required by economic theory, they were wished into existence. In such a market, all necessary information is in the hands of all players, who make well-informed decisions based on their own perceptions of the market's worth and meaning, driving prices to the 'correct' market level. Sadly, this is not true. There's a fundamental reason: 'human nature.' As the naturalist E.O. Wilson – a founder of sociobiology, and a leading researcher on ants – noted of Marxism: "Nice theory. Wrong species."

Picking holes in the concepts of fair markets would entail a book all of its own. But let us sow the following doubts in your mind:

- Not *all* information is in the hands of all players at the same time. For example, the SEC requires companies disseminating financial information to release it simultaneously to all news media. This being held impracticable, they are allowed to release it to a scattering of widely syndicated news outlets such as Reuters, Dow Jones, etc. The rate at which such information reaches 'all' media is variable, especially since fee-based services are also involved in dissemination of some information.

- Not all players in a market are working from the same viewpoint or specific knowledge. A buyer of fuel may be a utility or an industrial company buying for the 'burner tip,' or a financial

POWER MARKET RISK

institution buying as a 'hedge' against clients' loans. Or a pure speculator. A seller may be an oil company, a middleman (trader or agent) or any number of other entities. Each does not have the same motivation, viewpoint or financial position. A refiner may be selling surplus stocks of crude, knowing his refinery is taking a maintenance outage. There are many forms of 'inside knowledge,' quite legal to keep to oneself. In theory, all this should work itself out, but it may not do so when one or two players transact large volumes. It's proved relatively impossible for any single entity to 'corner' energy markets, but they certainly have the ability to sway the numbers short-term.

- Not all information is factual. A rumor is information in this sense. So is an imprecise report. This extends to prices, which can be rounded, romanticized, misreported or just plain rigged, as we shall see later.

- For a market to be completely fair, it needs *liquidity,* meaning a sufficiently large number of buyers and sellers, and a significant volume of product available for both 'spot' and for futures transactions. It needs *fungibility,* which means that individual 'parcels' or blocks traded have the same characteristics and are fully interchangeable. This is perfectly true when you're buying or selling 5,000 shares of Microsoft. But barrels of crude oil may vary greatly in quality, and are thus benchmarked against standard definitions such as Brent, Saudi Light, West Texas Intermediate, or some other commonly accepted standard. However, the specifications are somewhat loose, and often the subject of contention. The same applies to many oil products.

In the real world, then, we have to accept markets as 'fair enough,' since perfection is not available. Having made that assumption, in the risk community we have to decide what 'fair enough' means. Are some markets 'safe,' while others are inadvisable? Or are all of them risky to some extent? And if so, what is the correct viewpoint from a risk management standpoint?

Since real money is at stake, this is not some theological or abstract matter like 'how many angels can dance on the head of a pin?' You have to have your eyes open, and base your practices on common sense interpretations of market behavior. Markets inherently have no conscience, and no participant is buying or selling there for purely altruistic reasons.

Price Bubbles

Let's turn away from theory – always a good direction in which to turn – and instead address the blunt question: *"What the hell happened in California?"* Now, there's a topic of direct importance to electric utilities, if ever there was one!

Regrettably, the answer is 'we can't be 100% sure, we can only guess at some of it.' However, those guesses can be *informed* guesses, and help risk managers think about future behavior, since regretting past mistakes is not likely to prove anything but counter-productive. What happened in California and other western states is highly germane to risk managers. The saga is full of object lessons.

As longtime observers of the energy markets, we find it slightly comical to watch media reactions to the unfolding revelations about some of the events that occurred during the California crisis, especially to accounts of devious behavior by some of the participants. Rather than being 'shocked ... shocked!' at tales of market-rigging and manufactured shortages, we find that occurrences in the electricity market very closely parallel those we have observed in times of great upheaval or opportunity in other sectors.

First, let's start with some background. Vexed by paying higher electricity prices than competitors in other regions of the US, major consumers lobbied hard to have California deregulate, and a law passed in 1995 permitting importation of merchant power from other regions. California's Public Utilities Commission (PUC) carried out deregulation in a way that set it up to fail. It's notable that no other state that has deregulated has suffered anything like the problems seen in California.

The 1996 system allowed for consumer rates to be cut 10%, then to be frozen for five years. Utilities were turned into middlemen, being forced to sell their power plants, and left to buy power on the merchant market. Anyone could act as a merchant, or own the California power plants.

POWER MARKET RISK

Two agencies were formed to run the market. The California Power Exchange (CPE) set hourly prices for electricity, based on auctions conducted the day before the delivery. The California Independent System Operator (ISO) was set up to run the transmission lines. It also ran its own auctions for last-minute adjustments in supply and demand. For a while, everything worked as intended, with power costs below the fixed consumer rates.

But if you think about the way electricity demand works, you'll see that ISO was the weak link. To ensure the reliability it was charged with, it had to pay power plant operators to have units on standby to cover last-minute surges (surpluses not mattering, of course.) It was easy for circumstances to turn this mechanism into a sellers' market.

Nothing much happened until the spring of 2000, when water levels at hydroelectric dams in the Pacific Northwest – a source of about a fifth of California's summer power supply – ran low. Steady increases in demand had also chewed into the power surplus. Suddenly, there wasn't one. The prices charged for stand-by power jumped accordingly.

Seeing a sellers' market, producers were in a position to raise rates, and to be reticent about how much power they offered for sale. By June, Power Exchange investigations charge, supplies were being held back, held for sale to ISO, or sold out-of-state, or plants were idled to boost prices. It's been hard to figure out, since CPE and ISO records remain confidential. The blackouts started as utilities struggled to pay their power bills. Although many trading companies get blamed, Enron was the biggest offender, with schemes such as its 'Death Star' and 'Get Shorty' trading gambits, using chains of transactions.

Despite efforts by ISO, it couldn't stop the numerous games available for market players to use. According to a

POWER MARKET RISK

report in the *Wall Street Journal* (Sept. 16, 2002, p.1): "Enron bolstered its California operations [where it owned no power plants] by agreeing to manage electricity trades for other Western utilities, from Texas's El Paso Electric Co. to Valley Electric Association, a small cooperative in rural Parumph, NV. 'Everyone in the world thought these were the smartest people who ever lived,' says Gary Hedrick, chief executive of El Paso Electric, whose trading profits increase sevenfold to $22 million in 2001."

The problem reached the San Diego area first, where retail rates were uncorked in July 1999, to screams from customers. Elsewhere in California, ratepayers were oblivious, even though the utilities were losing money at a phenomenal rate every day. The California legislature re-regulated San Diego rates, and ISO tried price caps. Asked to intervene, the Federal Energy Regulatory Commission (FERC) saw no evil, at least none worth ascribing blame or requiring sellers to offer refunds.

Then the dominos really started to fall. Californian generating plants began to get sick – overworked or just a coincidence? – and maintenance outages increased. In November 2000, natural gas prices ballooned to four times that of a year before. Natural gas is the dominant fuel for power plants in environment-conscious California. It's alleged that supplies were deliberately squeezed to achieve this. Soon prices reached a level where power plants couldn't afford to meet ISO's capped price. Eventually, ISO had to abandon capped prices, and the PUC allowed a temporary 10% rate increase in January 2001. A fresh wave of blackouts in Northern and Central California followed, on orders from ISO to PG&E. Mid-month, Governor Gray Davis ordered the state's Department of Water Resources to take on power purchasing to keep the state running.

POWER MARKET RISK

Market games continued; on one day gas prices increased 33%. By March the State had agreed to $43 billion worth of deals, some lasting up to 20 years, to keep power flowing. Not well-structured, these deals led to the State selling power at a loss in slack times, and still gasping at the peaks. By April, Davis gave up and allowed a further 30% rate hike to stop the utilities going bankrupt. It didn't do the trick, and PG&E filed for bankruptcy protection. By June, it was 'all over': gas prices fell, hydro supplies recovered, and wholesale prices slid away, leaving some folks very much the richer from the spree. Remember, Enron went broke because of the stock market's lack of faith in the company after accounting irregularities were exposed. It's doubtful their trading operations lost them any money at all.

All's well that ends well? Probably not, because the underlying problems remain unsolved. California still lacks adequate generating capacity, and 'not in my back yard (NIMBY)' environmentalist activism may keep things that way.

Could it happen again? Maybe, although the chief 'villains of the piece,' as identified by accusers, have been badly mauled and may be inclined to think better of playing fast and loose in California, and perhaps other markets. But then, there's always human nature to take into account.

FERC Starts Excavating

Following Enron's bankruptcy, the hunt for justice (or, at least, blame) began. After accusations about unusual or manipulated price moves by consultant Robert McCullough before the US Senate Energy & Natural Resources Committee in January 2002, a persuasive conspiracy theory developed in the minds of many observers. If Enron had been engaged in shifty business practices in one segment of its business, was it not possible that it was 'up to no good' in energy pricing and supply for the hard-pressed California utilities?

Seeking to get to the bottom of this accusation, FERC carried out an extensive study of the 'price bubble,' paying particular attention to what is called 'price formation.' This term refers to the mechanisms by which sales and purchases, as construed by the marketplace in general, become definitive, and serve as benchmarks for that day's trades, or for future transactions. It also concerns itself with the topic of 'price discovery.' Shorn of economic jargon, it addresses the vexing question of 'what is the price of something, anyway?' And, how do we know? FERC's intent was to figure out how much prices had been rigged in the October 2000 through June 2001 period, and decide on how much should be refunded.

As you will see, the price of energy is not something that's written on a tag that can be scanned at the checkout counter, nor is it as sluggishly invariant as some industrial staple like, say, soda ash or sand. Because of active buying and selling interest, the price of electricity can vary almost by the second. Certainly, it will fluctuate to a greater or lesser extent within a matter of minutes, now that trading is carried out in real time on electronic systems, or by phone. That stands to reason, with surges in demand, flat spots, and unexpected outages or transmission difficulties.

McCullough may have overstated his case, somewhat. McCullough claimed forward electricity prices at Mid-Columbia had fallen by about 30% after the announcement of Enron's filing for bankruptcy on December 2. The implication of Dr. McCullough's testimony was that Enron had manipulated the market, causing prices to exceed market levels, and its bankruptcy then led to prices falling to considerably lower levels. "While Dr. McCullough claimed a 30% price drop, his own chart supported a smaller decline," says FERC, which added: "On February 4, 2002, an article in *Platt's Power Markets Week,* stated that the price drop was, in fact, not as large as McCullough reported, but was only about 9%..."

FERC's initial report about its investigations (issued in August 2002) said there are "specific instances of *possible* misconduct by three Enron affiliates and two investor-owned utilities that did business with Enron. The Enron companies are Enron Power Marketing Inc., Enron Capital & Trade Resources Corp, and Portland General Electric Co. The two other companies are Avista Corp., a Spokane, WA-based electric utility and El Paso Electric, an electric utility based in El Paso, TX." [Emphasis in the original] But as for McCullough's bubble, FERC believes it represents normal seasonality, which, with hindsight, seems more probable.

But it wasn't just these companies that were frowned on in the preliminary report. The report also said: "Publishers of electricity and natural gas price indexes use reporting methodologies without statistically valid sampling or information-verification procedures. While [FERC] is still evaluating whether there was any manipulation of published spot prices for natural gas, [there are] 'preliminary indications' that manipulation *may have* occurred. [FERC] also concludes that market participants had an 'incentive' to manipulate prices reported in published indexes." [Emphases in original] It also said it was puzzled by the different prices reported in late November by Bloomberg and Platt's.

Digging deeper, FERC said: "Enron Online was potentially susceptible to manipulation and was a significant source of price discovery for both market participants and publishers of energy pricing data."

And, confirming many an observer's suspicions of skullduggery, FERC observes: "Many of Enron's trading strategies involved deceit, including the provision of false information. [FERC investigators recommend] the Commission specifically prohibits submission of false information, or the omission of material information, in tariffs granting authority to sell wholesale power at market rates. This would make any revenues garnered with the help of false information or omission of material data subject to refund."

In other words, *'behave like good children, and play nicely.'*

Failure Of Oversight

Is FERC really up to the job? The Senate Government Affairs Committee concluded in a report issued on November 12, 2002 that the agency had too few staff working on enforcement, and that it had missed several clues about earlier Enron hanky-panky involving special purpose entities – in the wind power business – in the late 1990s.

Reading the Committee's report, it appears that FERC was asleep at the wheel throughout the California crisis, and was unduly influenced by Enron. The Senate said FERC was: "an agency that was no match for a determined Enron and that it has yet to prove that it is up to the challenge of proactively overseeing changing markets. On a number of occasions, FERC was provided with sufficient information to raise suspicions of improper activities – or had itself identified potential problems – in areas where it had regulatory responsibilities over Enron, but failed to understand the significance of the information or its implications. Over and over again, FERC displayed a striking lack of thoroughness and determination with respect to key aspects of Enron's activities – an approach seemingly embedded in its regulatory philosophy, regulations, and practices. In short, the record demonstrates a shocking absence of regulatory vigilance on FERC's part and a failure to structure the agency to meet the demands of the new, market-based system that the agency itself has championed."

FERC had plenty of opportunity to regulate the Enron family. As the Committee notes: "Although FERC does not directly regulate Enron Corp. (essentially a holding company for the company's many and diverse operating subsidiaries) as a corporation, *per se*, the Commission has jurisdiction over many of Enron's energy marketing, generation, and transmission subsidiaries and activities. In response to [our] request, FERC identified 24 electricity marketers, generators or transmitters, 15 gas pipelines, and 5 oil pipelines that are Enron subsidiaries or affiliates and that either are so-called 'jurisdictional entities' under the FPA, Natural Gas Act or Interstate Commerce Act or are QFs [qualifying facilities] that must be certified by FERC under PURPA [Public Utility Regulatory Policies Act]. In addition, Enron appears to have several other electric affiliates that are subject to FERC's jurisdiction or certification requirements."

Enron Online should have made FERC sit up and take notice. Says the Committee: "In October 1999, Enron launched an internet-based electronic trading platform, Enron Online, to trade natural gas and electric power and, later, other commodities. Online energy trading quickly became a significant portion of the energy trading market: in 2001, it was estimated to account for approximately 38% of natural gas and 17% of electric power marketed in the US; at the time, these figures were projected to grow to 72% for natural gas and 45% for electric power by 2005. Until Enron's bankruptcy, Enron Online was widely acknowledged to be the leading platform for such

POWER MARKET RISK

trading. Despite these developments in online trading, FERC appears initially to have been largely indifferent to their significance."

After the crisis was essentially over, FERC woke up and started an inquiry, in May 2001. As the Committee puts it: "The [FERC] report found that, unlike some online trading platforms which operate as third-party, 'many-to-many' exchanges matching willing buyers and sellers, Enron Online operated as a proprietary extension of Enron's trading units, including entities regulated by FERC. In other words, in this so-called 'one-to-many' exchange, an Enron trader was a party, either as a buyer or seller, to every trade on Enron Online. Therefore, only Enron would know valuable information about the actual volumes and prices transacted on its trading platform – and, of course, how the prices charged in any particular transaction were set or how they compared to those charged in other, similar transactions."

Since Enron Online was merely an asset-less 'trading platform,' the financial health of Enron as a whole was critical to the exchange's survival. In the Senate Committee's words, FERC decided that: "Enron did not have sufficient market share to disrupt the energy market if it failed. According to the report, Enron accounted for 16% of gas trading and 13% of electric power trading in North America, with the majority of Enron's trading transacted through Enron Online. In the report's view, the energy market could continue functioning smoothly absent Enron's market share. Second, the report concluded that, in any event, the chance of Enron failing financially was remote. The report provided little support for this conclusion."

"Finally, the report found that Enron Online gave a competitive advantage to Enron's own trading units by reducing their transaction costs, giving them wider access

POWER MARKET RISK

to the market, and providing them better market intelligence, but concluded that there was no reason for concern."

"In short, though the report identified a number of areas that ought to have troubled FERC as the federal government's lead energy regulator, it found no reason for concern and no cause for action. This was a critical mistake."

Darn right!

Really Rigged

It's not all 'suspicions' about market rigging. There are confessions, too. In October 2002, Enron vice-president Timothy Belden pleaded guilty to manipulation of prices in western markets, for which he was responsible. In his plea agreement, Belden acknowledged that between 1998 and 2001, he and "other individuals at Enron agreed to devise and implement a series of fraudulent schemes" in the California market that were designed to "obtain increased revenue for Enron from wholesale electricity customers and other market participants..." Enron wasn't alone. Several companies – American Electric Power, Dynegy, Williams Cos., CMS Energy Corp. and El Paso Corp. – have admitted that their traders provided manipulated data to Platt's and other reporting services.

Even FERC discovered, belatedly, what was going on. As the Senate Committee's report phrases it: "FERC staff's 2002 report on the Western energy markets describes one case where Enron and an unidentified counter-party made 174 trades with each other on Enron Online in a single day for natural gas being delivered into the California market at the height of the energy crisis. Other users of Enron Online, however, could only see the bid and ask prices for these transactions; they could not see that the same parties were involved in all of these trades. The net effect of these trades – which, the FERC staff report notes, took place at higher prices than trades with other parties – was to increase the price throughout the day. Though FERC staff stopped short of affirmatively concluding that Enron was attempting to use Enron Online to manipulate market data, it found in its 2002 report that the level of trading activity was "difficult to rationalize as normal or standard business practice."

On November 15, 2002, *The Wall Street Journal* revealed that it had winkled a report out of FERC, confirming that officials of Williams and AES Corp had also colluded to drive up prices during April-May 2000. Tape recorded conversations that fell into FERC's hands show that employees "discussed purposely prolonging a maintenance shutdown at the AES Alamitos plant," one of a pair supplying energy in the Los Angeles area, under contract to Williams.

Investigators are not the only ones who allege market rigging. The Enron collapse has spawned dozens of lawsuits, and the phenomenon is spreading. In a recent development, a civil class action suit on behalf of shareholders was filed in federal court in Houston on November 21, 2002, alleging that El Paso offered its traders incentives, including $10,000 bonuses, if they could increase their trading volume on the Intercontinental Exchange, a rival system to EnronOnline. El Paso traders were encouraged to engage in wash trading, the suit (filed by former Coastal Corp chairman Oscar Wyatt) complaint said. The Intercontinental Exchange was set up in April 2000 and its owners reportedly include El Paso, Duke, Reliant, Mirant, AEP and Aquila. Lawyers for the plaintiff allege that energy companies with the heaviest trading volumes thought they would receive a larger stake in a planned initial public offering of the exchange, which was expected some time in 2002, but hadn't happened by mid-November.

None of this tale of market confusion should have come as a surprise to those with experience of other energy markets. Maintenance shutdowns often occur at serendipitous moments. There has been a constant suspicion that many producing, trading and refining companies spend a great deal of effort on trying to influence the published prices of crude oil and petroleum products in local and world markets. And publishers spend a lot of effort trying not to be hoodwinked.

Enron and cronies aside, what FERC describes is a market that was 'rigged,' and that probably could never have been more than marginally fair. In FERC's view, price reporting services' published numbers are dismissed as 'inappropriate ... to use' to figure out the scale of the California swindle and what these ailing or bankrupt companies will be forced to cough up. It says: "No independent entity, such as this Commission, can verify the published price data. This is due, in part, to the reporting firms' status as non-jurisdictional entities as well as their legitimate desire to protect the confidentiality of their sources. Without knowing the source of the raw data, there cannot be any independent verification of the price data published by any reporting firm."

The 'Price' Issue

One might then conclude, if in a cynical frame of mind, and fully accepting of FERC's arguments: 'Well, what use at all are the third-part reporting services published numbers? What are they reporting, if not 'the price?' Some form of marketplace Muzak?' That's not true. Generally speaking, industry has placed a lot of reliance on published numbers, and has been confident of their relative accuracy.

Price reporting services are stuck between a rock and a hard place. Often relatively understaffed compared to the task they take on, they rely on telephone canvassing to deduce 'the price,' by talking to marketplace participants. It's a methodology that worked very well in slower days, but with the rise of screen-based real-time trading, it's a rather shaky basis for certainty. Even if every source were 100% truthful, there is plenty of scope for error. What is a 'price'? An average of the day's business? The price at close of trading? A subjective average based on a consensus of views? Reporters, to date at least, never get to view objective proof of what they hear, in the form of invoices or receipts. And – not to flog a dead horse – people will just flat out lie, to make a number conform to their own positions.

The reporting services FERC address include not only Platt's (*Gas Daily* and *Inside FERC Gas Market Reports*), but Bloomberg, Natural Gas Intelligence (NGI; *Daily Gas Price Index* and *Weekly Gas Price Index*), and Energy Intelligence Group (*Natural Gas Week*.) Bloomberg has had no official reaction to the FERC comments.

In an October 9, 2002 reply to FERC's August interim report, Platt's hotly dismissed most of the commission's concerns. It notes that: "Experts such as the California Energy Commission attributed the California price spike to a number of factors that the [FERC] report does not analyze: little excess interstate pipeline transportation capacity to California, exacerbated by the August 2000 rupture on El Paso Natural Gas; insufficient intrastate pipeline takeaway capacity; abnormally low levels of storage gas held by the California utilities heading into the winter of 2000-01; low hydropower availability; extremely cold weather in November 2000; and, according to some parties, actions taken by El Paso Merchant Energy and El Paso Natural Gas in managing pipeline capacity to California (the subject of rulings by an administrative judge.)"

Says Platt's editorial vice-president James Nicholson in this reply: "Platts ... does not agree with the conclusory nature of [FERC's] report in the absence of specific facts – for example the assertion that a 'circularity in information source' and 'the lack of any external validation almost guarantee that errors would not be discovered and eliminated [by price reporting publications], and create an environment that facilitates, rather than discourages, manipulation and collusion.' Platt's believes that this claim is unfounded."

Nicholson makes a valid point when he adds: "Regardless of whether the California energy market was in fact manipulated, Platt's maintains that its assessments accurately reflected the market. Even if, for example, Enron did attempt to manipulate the California market through its buy/sell postings on [Enron Online], *that was the market*. Willing market participants did transactions at those prices, and Platt's (and it believes other publishers) accurately reported that dealmaking." He also concludes, quite correctly, "Platt's believes that any market is subject to attempted manipulation," as we can only agree.

To lay more than a minor portion of the blame on the price services, though, is to 'shoot the messenger,' albeit messengers who may be somewhat imprecise or naïve in their reporting.

Scott C. Speaker, editor-in-chief of *Natural Gas Week,* commented on FERC's interim report in an editorial. "Much of the business of journalism – including the trade press and price reporting services – is predicated on the concept of trust," he said. "We must establish a relation-

POWER MARKET RISK

ship and trust our sources to pass along quality information, and our readership must trust us to verify that information by whatever means possible and protect those readers from spin and manipulation." He also thinks: "the actual accuracy of a published index in providing the true snapshot of trading in a specific market is not really in question. The system isn't perfect, but is the best one we've got...and getting better. No commodity price reporting system -- aside from Commodity Futures Trading Commission-regulated futures and options exchanges -- provides fully verified and transparent prices." He termed FERC's ideas about pricing 'unrealistic.'

It's expected that the reporting services will try to refine their methods to address FERC and industry concerns. Platt's has called on energy companies to change their price disclosure methods, requesting more detailed price and trading data, certified by a senior executive, and originating outside the trading department. In some cases, this had already started to happen by mid-November 2002. It had to happen, after the role of traders in price manipulation became so publicly apparent, because a whole slew of companies had by then instructed their traders not to discuss pricing with reporters. That list may vary, but at the time included Royal Dutch/Shell's Coral Energy, Duke Energy Corp., Mirant Corp., Conectiv Energy and AEP, most of whom are issuing price data from their risk management offices, a highly appropriate move. But several others (again, as of mid-November) including Constellation Energy Group, El Paso, Reliant Resources Inc., PPL Corp., Williams and CMS have suspended price reporting altogether, according to Dow Jones Newswires.

Natural Gas Week published a list of seven improvements that it will make in its price reporting for its weekly indices. *NGW's* Speaker noted: "A common man-

POWER MARKET RISK

tra in the energy business is "the market works," and indeed the publishing sector is no different. For example, when industry-wide concerns were raised over California gas prices two years ago numerous regional gas buyers and sellers – large and small – subsequently answered the call to provide *NGW* additional spot and bid-week prices. This "market crisis" ultimately boosted the liquidity and breadth of *NGW's* indices in the western region, an improvement that carries forward to today. *NGW* expects the current crisis will lead to similar positive changes."

And perhaps something positive is already emerging. Speaker claims: "The efforts are already paying dividends. Despite the high-profile withdrawal of several large participants from the market over the past few months, *NGW* over this time has added several other Top 20 gas marketers to its survey and secured promises from several more – both old and new to our survey – that, once their internal reviews are satisfactorily completed, they will also provide data on a daily and monthly basis."

Why is reliable pricing information so important? For good or bad, market participants have come to rely on published indices rather than to simply strike deals based on their own intuitions about what is fair to both parties, for prompt or longer-term contracts. That's because management wants to see the prices a company pays or achieves compared to some benchmark, directly or through a formula, demonstrating that it has not been shortchanged. It's critical, therefore, that pricing information is seen to be accurate, and not swayed by manipulation.

The Real Blame

The blame for the California mess rests squarely on those who devised a poorly conceived deregulation plan, on a

POWER MARKET RISK

lack of enforcement, and on the aggressive behavior of trading companies, some of which crossed the line into market-rigging and collusion.

In early November, the US attorney's office in San Francisco began issuing grand jury subpoenas to trading companies active in the California market, seeking evidence. As well as criminal charges, these could lead to evidence on which California could base claims for restitution. Around that time, Williams Companies agreed to a $417 million settlement of claims with the state of California relating to events in 2000 and 2001, and agreed to restructure future power contracts.

The FERC investigation of the 2000-2001 power scandal is supposed to wrap up by February 2003. It's to be hoped that when it does, honest merchant energy suppliers can get back to rebuilding their businesses, which have suffered greatly since.

FERC is still looking into the effects of 'wash trading' – repeated back-and-forth trading at flat prices between parties to cause an illusion of greater transaction volumes – in conjunction with Commodities Futures Trading Commission (CFTC) and the Securities & Exchange Commission (SEC). And one of FERC's chief responses to the scandal has been to create a new Office of Market Oversight and Investigations (OMOI) dedicated specifically to oversee the electric and natural gas markets.

It seems highly probable that wash trading and 'daisy chains' – in which a parcel trades from hand-to-hand, and often with overlapping ownership, at increasing prices – played a major part in the California price bubble.

We've already noted that deregulation wasn't managed well in this instance. But there's a basic reason: clashing interests. A close observer comments: "I think everyone felt the regulator would protect consumers. And most of the decisions that firms made were predicated on that assumption. When that didn't happen, everything came unraveled. Restructuring hasn't worked in the US as it has in other countries because of our federal and state jurisdictional problems. The feds control the wholesale market and the states control the retail market. In order to have a market that benefits consumers and works, you've got to have coordination of retail policies with wholesale policies. There's not much love lost between federal and state regulators. That's unfortunate, because the only people hurt by that are the consumers."

"That's the big lesson - you must coordinate the two policies. You'll hear entities say, 'We need to let the demand play in the wholesale market.' That 's fine and good. But demand can't go play in the wholesale market, if it can't go play in the retail market. You can say we have price-responsive demand in the wholesale market. But unless you can actually send price signals to final customers on an hourly basis to get them to move away from these hours or interrupt them, forget it. It's not going to work."

So was deregulation simply a mistake? "Under the circumstances that it was done, I think yes," he continues. "But do I think that a restructured market can benefit consumers? Yes. Unfortunately, I still don't think that FERC has clued in to the purpose of restructuring as a benefit to consumers. If we don't restructure to benefit consumers, then it's very clear, as is happening right now, they will deny firms the capital to do what they need to do. And they will essentially make it very difficult on the legal side to continue restructuring."

"That would be a shame. But if consumers' interests aren't being served, the political process will work to prevent restructuring. One thing that hasn't been borne in mind is that we can always go back to regulation. That's certainly what consumers believe. That is an option. We can't just say we will have competition regardless of the cost, because people get angry."

Paper Tigers

What about the Commodity Futures Trading Commission (CFTC)? This body has (or had) oversight over all futures markets, financial and physical. It has developed a reputation as a 'paper tiger' over the years.

We hesitate to point a finger, or to accuse people of bad faith, but it is notable that CFTC recused itself from any role in these markets when it supported passage of Commodity Future Modernization Act (CFMA) in 2000. (Was this because of political influence or lobbying by Enron and others? Some say so.) And having done so, it didn't pay much attention while California suffered its blackouts.

Turning to Platts' Nicholson again: "if traders from whom Platt's obtained prices were using [Enron Online (EOL)] for price discovery, and if EOL had gained a dominant role in determining natural gas prices as a direct consequence of Congress's decision pursuant to [CFMA] to exempt trading systems such as EOL from regulation, that is an issue for federal legislators and regulators to address."

Although FERC is rapidly playing catch-up on the affairs of 200-2001, it has not shown itself to be a very responsive or effective regulatory body. Little of what FERC has learned in its investigations can be new to market participants, although FERC's findings will probably help clarify what were merely suspicions in the past. But FERC is only closing the stable door, long after the horse has bolted.

POWER MARKET RISK

Going forward, can we expect either CFTC or FERC to create a level playing field, as the jargon has it? They'll undoubtedly make some improvements, but the potential for abuse will always be present. And of course, that's why effective risk management is so important to the future health of the industry.

Bitter Lessons

Is there any risk management strategy that could have saved Californian utilities? When you consider the staggering volumes of gas and electricity involved over the period of the crisis, perhaps not as much as utilities would have liked. But a well-planned RM strategy could certainly have done a lot to ease the pain.

To be fair, who could have built sufficient hedges against such trends, or more important, even thought to do so? At least, at the time: after all, the promise of deregulation was lower prices, and initially, that's what happened. Lulled into a false sense of security, a policy of short-term buying developed, and a fear of long-term contracts arose. After all, why be left paying way over the market for power? When such a mindset develops, it takes a paradigm shift to alter it.

So what do you, as a more or less willing participant in markets, do? Do you say, *'Well it's like death and taxes. It's inevitable, I have to do business through some form of trading system, on some sort of market, don't I?'*

In a sense, this is not a cop-out, but the right answer. To take full advantage of all the sources of supply and outlets, you have to be a player to play. But that doesn't mean you have to join in mutual suicide pacts, by participating in illiquid or suspicious trading arenas! If you suspect a market is being manipulated, speak up. Complain to regulators. File lawsuits.

POWER MARKET RISK

Deregulated arenas are particularly dangerous. "The operating risk that companies face in a deregulated environment today far overshadows the current market risk from trading activities. But, that's not how people view it," says G. Patrich Simpkins, CRO of TWU.

A lot of deregulation-influenced factors, and the underlying nature of the Californian market, also came into play in 2000-2001. One distinguished observer, who declining to be identified by name, said: "The big thing to remember is the closer to delivery you purchase your power, the more opportunities there are to get nailed. If you wait until you are close to delivery, the number of potential suppliers to provide power is smaller. So the likelihood you could have to pay very high prices for power is greater. Plan in advance as much as you can. Because the further back in time you make your purchases, the more competitors there are to provide electricity, and the better your chances that you'll get a good deal."

There's a good analogy for this, he reasons: "You don't buy health insurance on the spot market. You contract in advance for health care. If you don't, when you arrive at the hospital with a broken arm and ask the doctors to fix it, you may get stuck with very high payment."

"Competition in this market takes place at fairly long horizons. That's the fundamental problem. The market isn't very deep at very short horizons. The firms that are supplying that market don't want it to be very deep. So your job as a buyer is to plan to purchase as little as possible in short-term markets. That's really the key."

How can an energy company protect itself against price manipulation? "The best thing you can do is understand the markets your company is selling or buying in, the weakness these markets have, get numerous price quotes, diversify your base of creditable counterparties, and in addition to measuring market and credit risk, understand the associated political risk associated with each of the markets you are exposed to, and avoiding over reliance on any one price index or any non-representative price indices," contends Mark Williams, Risk Management Expert at the Finance And Economics Department of Boston University.

We'd suggest that NYMEX, CME and international exchanges like IPE or LIFFE are probably a very good risk, based on past history. It can be argued that their closing prices are objective, rather than subjective. There is liquidity – the daily trading volume is validated and published by the exchanges – and there's a great deal of oversight.

Beware of all other trading arenas! Test them for liquidity! It seems unfathomable to us that so many would have relied on a system like Enron Online during the period in question, when it was obvious that Enron could have been playing both sides of the market, and when it dominated the liquidity of the system. A market where one player predominates is *not* liquid, whatever the transaction volume.

And what about those price services? Whatever market you're working in, it might be wise to use more than one to base your deals on, if you decide to use such a mechanism to set prices retroactively or arbitrate disagreements. First of all, make certain you understand the methodology used, and exactly what the prices represent. To obtain that information, talk directly to the staff of the publication. *Don't* rely on what someone else in the market says about what the prices represent. That person may not be giving you correct information.

Interact with the pricing services in another way: Call them with your ten cents' worth when cognitive dissonance strikes you. You can be sure that counter-parties and others with an axe to grind have done so. Have a lit-

POWER MARKET RISK

tle sympathy, though: price reporting is a soul-destroying and thankless task, involving making rapid judgments about the veracity of market chatter, from a spectrum of participants, not all of whom are scrupulously honest, nor unmotivated by their own self-interest.

And finally, don't lie to reporters. There are two good reasons: one is ethical. The second is self-interest: if your account of what's happening isn't regarded as trustworthy, you lose your opportunity to refine the process of price discovery.

It seems prudent to us that those who propose to use third-party information to set contract prices or base deals should carefully study how those prices, historically, have tracked with their own experience. If they find good correlation, then, to borrow a term from the food/pharmaceutical industry, the information can be deemed 'Generally Recognized As Safe' for a specific purpose.

Users should also pay particular attention to how those prices react in times of volatility, again comparing them with their own intuitions and experience. In following this course, they will be able to reach a deeper understanding of how to formulate their contracts, whether by using some form of multi-day time-average, 'spreads' or combination of prices from competing services, weighted or unweighted, to hedge their risk. It's merely commonsense risk management, when so much money rides on deals.

Chapter 12:

The Apple Of Temptation: Run An Honest Business

Corporate governance. It's one of those eye-glazingly dull phrases. A real page-turner. But, it has an important part to play in making risk management work.

We've dwelled on 'rogue traders,' and they really do exist. We've also talked about 'rigged markets,' and have seen that there's every reason to suppose that these, too, are an ongoing problem. Lawmakers and enforcement agencies perceive white-collar crime to be a growing phenomenon in the US, although perhaps we are merely seeing a greater awareness of it, and a greater rate of discovery of offenders.

But what about 'crooked companies'? Depending on how you define 'crooked,' there have been quite a few exposed, just lately. Besides Enron, fingers have been pointed at a number of other trading operations. And then there's Tyco, WorldCom, Adelphia, a growing list ... Some of these operations were involved in 'accounting problems' that should have been spotted, and prevented, by proper risk management strategies.

POWER MARKET RISK

Now, here's an even more scary thought. What if your management methods, too, are guilty of creating an environment in which your *own* company may encourage the proliferation of unethical and risk-generating habits? The mere thought of this will probably make most readers throw up their hands in horror, and repeat the mantra: *"No, no, it can't happen here! Not at BobCo Power! We are s-o-o clean!"*

Don't be so sure.

Here's a checklist of signs to watch for:

- An obsession with ever-rising quarterly earnings, 'no matter what.'
- A 'jock culture' that rewards swaggering behavior, cutting of corners, and sharp dealing.
- Senior executives who do not take the corporate code of conduct seriously, or who shrug, or wink, and say 'yes, but …' when ethical questions are raised.
- An obsession with image, brand and marketing over quality, customer satisfaction and reliability.
- A proliferation of subsidiaries, partnerships and other vehicles rather than a logical, compartmented corporate structure.
- Signs of 'celebrity management' or personality cults

The subject here is, sad to say, *hypocrisy* rather than just plain old-fashioned crime. It makes no difference at all, at the end of the day, if a corporation has a bold Mission Statement full of right-sounding words, or a code of conduct that prohibits ethical transgressions, if no one takes them seriously.

Guidance has to come from the top. But it can't be in the form of empty words. Codes of conduct can only

mean something if there is both executive-level and board-level support for their enforcement, and the company-wide perception that they *mean something* and will be *applied across the board.*
Here's a finely crafted set of company guidelines or 'core values' to study:

> **Respect.** We treat others as we would like to be treated ourselves. We do not tolerate abusive or disrespectful treatment. Ruthlessness, callousness and arrogance don't belong here.
> **Integrity.** We work with customers and prospects openly, honestly and sincerely. When we say we will do something, we will do it; when we say we cannot or will not do something, then we won't do it.
> **Communication.** We have an obligation to communicate. Here, we take the time to talk with one another ... and to listen. We believe that information is meant to move and that information moves people.
> **Excellence.** We are satisfied with nothing less than the very best in everything we do. We will continue to raise the bar for everyone. The great fun here will be for all of us to discover just how good we can really be.

Now, who could argue with that?

It's motherhood and apple pie.

Sadly, though, these were the widely circulated, constantly emphasized 'core values' of Enron Corp.

No doubt a large proportion of the workforce treated

them with due seriousness. In the end, it didn't matter a bit, because senior executives didn't, having developed their own private culture of 'anything goes,' and 'my house is bigger than yours,' and 'anything to get the bonus.' Even though the company's accompanying code of ethics ran to a 64-page book, and required all employees to sign an annual compliance agreement, the train still ran off the tracks.

How? It's simple. In corporations, employees learn that what the management wants is what the management gets. It's a question of survival. When there are mixed, or hidden signals, human nature will quickly divine what is 'really wanted,' and people will begin to act accordingly, willingly or otherwise.

Is this pure cynicism? No, it's not.

The Board of Directors

Directors are selected and appointed with the idea that they are the representatives of the shareholders. In a period of greed, such as the one we have (presumably) recently survived and transcended, 'shareholders wishes' are often interpreted to mean, 'make me as much money as you can, though higher stock prices and dividends.'

The value placed upon individual classes of stockholders can become skewed – Wall St. analysts and bankers are particularly adept at identifying their own views with those of all shareholders, and they have a louder voice. It's up to directors to act as the 'conscience' of a corporation.

They are not paid their fees simply to turn up every few months for a convivial lunch, to be schmoozed, to watch a series of PowerPoint presentations, and to hear only the management side of the story, then glibly rubberstamp it as policy. Directors should play an active role in understanding how ethical issues are treated, and how the corporation actually works.

Ideally, directors should be chosen from a wider network of possible candidates. All too often, the same types of shopworn corporate retirees, politicians, academics, golfing buddies and 'look-alikes' seem to populate boards. Boards should consist of a broad spectrum of interests, even including corporate gadflys and activists. Some more youthful participation is needed throughout corporate America.

One of the greatest concerns of directors should be risk management, in the broadest sense of the word: the risks of acquisitions, of diversification, of new marketing ideas, of financial strategy, of trading posture, of capital investments. Assumptions should be questioned, and the risk staff invited to address the board directly.

That's not to say that the stage should be set for innovations to be crushed by dull gray conservatism, but instead that fresh ideas should be given a fair chance.

If a new business concept promises a 15% annual growth rate and good margins, let the proponents explain and defend their assumptions, and show that there's a well-developed risk management strategy associated with it.

Directors should probe to discover the roots of the idea: Is this just a 'pet project'? What if it goes wrong? What's the downside? What are the marketplace risks, and ethical issues? Are these numbers, real? How were they developed? What's the statistical validity?

These are all questions that a wide-awake board can get addressed, and answered.

With the right board, and the right attitude, most corporate problems will be solved. The tone has to come 'from the top.'

POWER MARKET RISK

The Management Committee

Here, we hold a very old-fashioned viewpoint: From the CEO on down, senior managers are *employees*. Just because there has been a movement towards rewarding them lavishly with stock options – to the extent that they may think *they* are the most important shareholders – nothing changes this fact. The idea of options is to align the interests of managers and shareholders, taking them from mere custodians to active players in enriching those who have staked their savings on a company's ability to perform.

Senior executives are responsible for setting an ethical and responsible tone. This doesn't mean they have to wear sackcloth suits from Sears and drive 1995 Buicks, but it does mean that they need to avoid setting themselves up as princelings and celebrities. People who aspire to 'show biz' money should be in show biz. It's no use saying 'we have to pay astronomical salaries to attract the best talent.' It's simply not true. What did the talent and genius of Jeffrey Skilling or Andrew Fastow do for Enron, as one simple example? Companies should be managed by people who will do a fair day's work for a fair day's pay, and not prima donnas, con men or tyrants.

Human Resources

HR people shouldn't allow themselves to be corralled into merely being the 'hiring and firing details' people, or the enforcers of political correctness. HR should work closely with the executive committee to make sure ethical issues and problems are addressed in a consistent way. And that support is given to enforcing these guidelines by managers, and on managers.

It's not enough to hold regular in-house 'consciousness

raising' seminars. Is the message being conveyed in other ways? Do HR people take complaints about unethical behavior or suspicious business practices seriously? Meaning, as seriously as they take complaints about racial slurs, homophobia, or sexual harassment? Are offenders seen to face consequences?

Make It Stick

Part of the curse of 'guidelines' is that employees – including senior management – quickly come to see them as just that, mere suggestions and social pressure. It would be much wiser if they were called something more definitive like 'rules' or 'commandments.'

Many psychological studies have suggested that the majority of humans will lie, steal or cheat given the opportunity, if the rewards are great enough, and the risk is low enough. The history of the 20th Century tells us a lot about what societies will lure their citizens into doing, and a corporation is, after all, a microcosmic society.

You've already gone to great lengths in your organization – we hope – to eliminate transparently dishonest employees and to avoid hiring ones whose past records and behavior lead to the suspicion of future dishonesty. But you cannot afford to make the assumption that either white-collar crime, or counterproductive thuggish behavior, will not ferment, and negatively affect your business.

You have to take steps to discourage it at every step: through firm rules, error-proof procedures and oversight, and by developing an underlying corporate culture that won't support damaging or irresponsible behavior.

Chapter 13:

How Risk Management Can Save the Day

We've heard a lot of horror stories since Enron went under – think of all the companies that were adversely affected by Enron's demise because of their large credit exposure. But what about the companies that weathered the storm, because their risk management program and CROs responded quickly to the threat? Yes, they do exist. American Electric Power (AEP) is one of them.

One of the reasons AEP was able to survive the threat posed by Enron is because the company practices risk management. The company has an enterprise risk management program, headed by Scott Smith, CRO. Smith is a no-nonsense kind of guy. He is strict about the company and employees adhering to AEP's risk management principles. You don't negotiate with Smith about risk management.

Says Smith: "I think some people are surprised at how seriously risk management is taken at AEP. There are no negotiations when you get over certain limits. We lost $60 million in gas in the first quarter [of 2002]. And one analyst said, 'You should fire the risk management team.' However, I explained that the $60 million loss was the result of the limit structure in place. The traders went outside of those limits, and it cost them money. A large proportion of our losses are the result of our limit structure in which there was no negotiation. The traders knew that. The senior management knew that. We had to get back within limits," Smith comments.

"The top of the trading organization consists of people of high integrity," notes Smith. "They understand the game rules, they understand the importance of risk management, and they understand they have to get back within the limits. When they are out of bounds, there's no 'let's go negotiate with Scott.' It's a disciplined approach where are there are no ifs, ands, or buts. That in itself has addressed the market volatility issues," says Smith.

The combination of an enterprise-wide program and strict adherence to the principles of that program really benefited AEP when the energy markets began to fall apart as Enron crumbled. From the Chairman of the Board all the way down the line, AEP's employees understand the value of risk management. "If you look across the industry, AEP is a pretty large player. I'm proud to say that we've come out unscathed from these scandals that are happening," Smith says. "Enron was our largest credit exposure. When the risk management committee, consisting of the chairman, the CEO and others across the corporation, met in September before Enron went down, we collectively said, 'The ballgame's over. We're done. We are going to start reducing our risks.'

"This was a strategy set out by the front office, legal, and risk management. The Chairman, the CFO, and COO were all onboard. It really worked effectively when on the Friday before Enron declared bankruptcy, Ken Lay called up my Chairman and said, 'You owe me money.' My Chairman turned around and said, 'No, you owe *me* money,' because he had the information."

POWER MARKET RISK

People knew what was going on: "Because we have an enterprise risk management approach, we were able to fan out across the corporation and say, 'We have all this risk with Enron.' That permeated out through the organization. For instance, we wouldn't pick up a barge load of coal at that time, because it would have increased our credit exposure with Enron. The barge captain knew enough about the situation to call us before he picked up the coal. We were able to knock down our exposure in a number of areas. In the three months from the time we met in September until Enron declared bankruptcy, we were able to whittle down our exposure considerably. We succeeded because we had the front office and risk management working together rather than against each other."

That willingness to work together carries over to all parts of AEP's operation. That's one of the strength's of the company's program. Everyone knows risk management is important. "I know the risk management group has made an impact on the corporation," comments Smith. "Recently, one of my colleagues was in London and overheard two AEP traders talking. One trader said, 'The only people we have to worry about is risk management. If we can get this approved by them, then it will pass.' I got a smile on my face, hearing that story."

At AEP, it's not just trading that has to pass contracts by risk management. It's other parts of the company, too. While risk management obviously saved the day during the Enron crisis, it can keep the company out of trouble during the normal course of everyday business, too. Risk management can help you stay out of a crisis as well as responding when you are under the gun. It means having an astute CRO that can spot the potential problem and avert disaster.

"When we embarked on the enterprise risk manage-

POWER MARKET RISK

ment approach, a lot of people thought it was a project, rather than a process." However, it's clear now that it is a process. In traditional risk management, the CRO is responsible for credit and market risk. But at AEP, using the enterprise risk management concept, Smith is also responsible for business and operation risk. And the various risk department work together to mitigate any potential risk problems. For instance, says Smith, "The engineering department wanted to do a major contract with a company that had been shut off as a counterparty on the trading desk. The engineering department was surprised that when I saw the name of the company, I didn't even review the contract. I said no to it. It didn't get sent to the Board."

Why does risk management work so well at AEP? According to Smith, "It comes down to the commitment, not lip service, of upper management and the board to risk management. I have full support of the board and senior management. It's very important to me to have that kind of support. Risk management is taken seriously here. It's not considered a nuisance."

While other companies may have risk management groups in place, they won't succeed unless they can act decisively. "A lot of risk management organizations fail, because they fail to act, Smith says. "If risk management is just a bunch of fancy models and guys with PhDs, it's not worth a hill of beans if you don't do something with it. There's an over reliance on models. I try to use common horse sense versus just strictly relying on what a VAR model says."

Managing Trust At Risk

Like AEP, TXU has a CRO, G. Patrich Simpkins, who oversees an enterprise risk management program. Like

POWER MARKET RISK

Smith, Simpkins has broad powers as CRO. As broad as those powers are, there is only one focus for them. Says Simpkins: "Our metric is: Trust At Risk. We don't want to put a lot of trust at risk." That's particularly important now as shareholders may be feeling distrustful of a company's intentions, thanks to Enron, Tyco and WorldCom.

According to Simpkins, "Right now, the middle office's role is to manage trust at risk. In order to do that, you should assess the limits and goals of the stakeholders, rather than the aspirations of the company. It's important to understand the tradeoffs between sexy and sure. Communications with stakeholders is essential. From TXU's standpoint, we understand the fiduciary and contractual obligation, and we drive home credibility and ethical conduct in our practices."

In order to keep trust, a company has to make certain its risk management operation runs smoothly and that all the risks facing the company are taken into consideration. Simpkins gives the following advice: "Regarding fundamentals, make sure the systems operate appropriately. Make sure your risk reporting is effective. Make sure the right policies are in place. Make sure there are limits in place and that they are understood. On the harder issues, make sure to manage cash, not just earnings. Cash flow risk is extremely important right now. Focus on credit risk and tie credit risk to market risk. Focus on operational risk and understand what those risks are. Understand what portfolio drivers and threats are and the impacts and the probability of those impacts."

How do you encompass all of those aspects in a risk management program? Here's how it's done at TXU:

"I have a global staff that, from a portfolio perspective, focuses on market, credit, operational risk" and strategic risk, Simpkins states. "Every region throughout the world has a middle office because of the specificity of each region, the types of businesses they are in, and the markets. If there are sub regions within a region, those sub regions have a specific risk manager. For example, TXU has offices in seven countries on three continents. We have three middle offices – in the US, in Australia, and in Europe. But in the case of Europe, we have subs in Geneva, in Stockholm, and in Germany. Each of those areas has a risk manager."

In addition, TXU has regional chief risk officers. "Reporting to them are risk officers for lines of business," Simpkins explains. "Then, we have local risk managers. Therefore, there is a person who has responsibility for generation, retail, trading and risk management. Within trading risk management, there are book managers. Therefore, risk managers run risk management for that group. Those risk managers have the responsibility for risk control, risk practices, risk systems, and risk analytics. Whatever it makes sense to centralize, we centralize. For example, consider a forward curve. The dynamics of how TXU structures a forward curve, the correlation matrix and the volatility matrix would be driven out of the global risk office. Application of that model is the responsibility of the risk management group at the regional level and the book manager level. The reason is there are nuances every single day in the market that affect that forward curve analysis. When a model is taken to a regional level and changes are made, there's a process involved called 'V in V' which is where we take the model, verify the changes, and affirm that the changes are appropriate. We have to be consistent so our risk reporting stays consistent.

"Something that's fairly unique to TXU, and has worked very well for us, is that all the middle offices heads are a direct solid line report to the global risk officer and also a direct solid line report to the regional

POWER MARKET RISK

group president," remarks Simpkins. "It might not work for every company, because a lot depends on the personalities and the understanding of roles and responsibilities. Tactically and operationally, the responsibility of that middle office head is really to that business unit president. My purview is strategic. Effectively, it's my prescribed mandate. But I have to look at the regional president as my customer. I think TXU tries very hard to develop a risk culture that embraces a process of collaboration, not consensus, between the front, middle, and back offices. If you asked me about TXU's successes, I would say setting up that dynamic and having it work appropriately, which I believe it does, and effectively having a cross-functional team to resolve particular issues is a huge success for us. A year ago, none of this existed. It's similar to if building the Empire State Building. You don't want to build a building of that scale on a six-inch slab. The piers should be driven deeply into the ground."

In Simpkins opinion, "TXU has done a good job putting policies and procedures in place. For example, someone in retail might have a customer that he wants to keep. He wants to create a new product for that customer. That product needs to be approved. But there are questions surrounding that product. Such as, 'How do we price it? What's the system we need to track it? How do we develop a confirmation process? How much of it are we going to sell? That determines the kind of system that we're going to use. What risk book will it be broken down into? How will it be managed?' If a company doesn't ask these questions, an operational risk may be created that can't be hedged. Many operational risks are systemic. The purpose of governance and policies is to mitigate these occurrences. To be honest, it doesn't work 100 percent of the time. But for TXU, it's 95 percent effective. The other 5 percent requires either education, or disciplinary actions, or tighter controls with respect to systems."

It's also important to monitor risk on an ongoing basis, Simpkins points out. "TXU has risk monitoring forums for every business unit. These forums have an operational-tactical responsibility. There are monthly reviews of everything that's transacted, whether it's new products, new markets, new contracts, and new opportunities. Those risk monitoring forums roll up to regional risk monitoring committees. Those regional risk-monitoring committees roll up to the global risk management committee, which comprises myself, the presidents of the various business units, the group presidents, and the chief financial officer. We meet every six weeks. The global risk management committee has two lines of responsibility. One is to the executive committee of the company. The other is to the audit committee of the board of directors. I chair and represent that committee for the audit committee of the board. I sit in with the executive committee on decisions about the company's portfolio and direction of the company's business, and what we're doing with strategy.

"Business, operational, credit, and market risk all tie together at some point and drive the portfolio value at risk. I think we have a good measure for this. One of the successes at TXU is not only having a good risk culture and good governance structure, but also being able to roll up those positions so that people are aware. It's also the openness of the risk culture. Anyone can raise his or her hand and ask for help with a problem. One thing that TXU has done down through the middle office, and that we continue to drive down, is that we have a fiduciary responsibility to the stakeholders of this company, first and foremost," he states.

While TXU has a good risk program in place, "we have our challenges, just like any company," Simpkins says. "How do we handle changing portfolio dynamics with a limited amount of risk capital? How do we drive best decisions and choices? The decisions we make today drive our tomorrow. If we misjudge what drives operational cash flow, we create a problem for ourselves down the road that becomes operational and tactical. We'll find ourselves putting out fires. Just like any company, we're not above putting out fires. The day we are through putting out fires, I'll know that we've been relatively successful.

"How do we measure success? When we look at risk and manage prospectively, when the board clearly understands risk management's role within the company and can relate that to shareholder interest and preferences, and when the profit and loss managers of the company say that risk management is an integral part of their process. If we can achieve that, then we'll be in the top percentile of companies regarding risk management.

"TXU is going to continue to be more successful in this business because the company has the right culture and management philosophy to make it possible. It always flows from the top. We have an outstanding chairman and chief executive, Erle Nye, who has created the right atmosphere to get things done and be successful. TXU has an atmosphere that encourages honesty. I think that's really important. The company has extremely high integrity. The company is frank with its board members and its stakeholders. Without that, you have no basis to build on," comments Simpkins.

Chapter 14:

Stemming The Tide of Stakeholder Discontent

In some ways, the Enron debacle hasn't been a bad thing for American business. We have finally put the glitzy years of the 1980s and 1990s behind us. Rather than looking for wild profits and soaring share prices from companies that might not be around next year, stakeholders are seeking to invest in companies that have some staying power and ethics.

Companies and organizations have seen the change in stakeholders expectations and are trying hard to win back stakeholder confidence. One of the ways to do that is by instituting standards in a number of areas of risk management. Those are the aims of two groups – the National Energy Marketers Association and the Committee of Chief Risk Officers (CROs).

NEM's Task Force

In response to the crisis of financial confidence in the energy markets, the National Energy Marketers Association (NEM) joined forces with Wall Street firms as well as with accounting and financial experts to draft an industry code for risk management and financial

POWER MARKET RISK

disclosures. The aim of the NEM Risk Valuation, Management and Accountability Task Force is to identify practices that will rebuild stakeholder confidence and stabilize energy markets.

These are critical areas from a risk management standpoint and must be addressed. Explains NEM President Craig Goodman: "What does it mean for risk management? If you take a look at what NEM is doing regarding risk management and financial governance, we have some very constructive guidelines that can help restore confidence and financial integrity to the energy markets. In my opinion, the market will force companies into best practices. The market is punishing bad actors far worse than regulators ever could. What regulator in the country has the power to fire CEOs and CFOs and to devalue corporations by 90% in a matter of weeks?"

Beginning in May 2002, Task Force teams worked on drafting suggestions with an eye to creating an industry consensus.

A discussion draft of the "Energy Market Stability Framework" was written in late June and covers six areas – disclosure, market risk, credit risk, capital adequacy, compliance, and governance. The draft framework thoroughly outlines these key areas, sets goals, and suggests ways to meet these goals.

"We feel we have come up with an outstanding discussion draft," comments Goodman. "NEM wants to ensure the financial integrity of the US energy markets. Otherwise, companies won't have the money to invest in needed infrastructure. We need financially healthy companies to keep the industry strong. We cannot finance the infrastructure of the 21st century with junk bonds."

What are the objectives? Let's take a look:

POWER MARKET RISK

Disclosure Objectives

- To improve transparency of information in critical areas so as to allow stakeholders to develop a more accurate understanding of business activities which create risk, and associated levels of return
- To identify information to be included in regular disclosures to market stakeholders

Market Risk Objectives

- To identify, standardize and require the tracking of key metrics which measure market risk
- To standardize the methodology for portfolio valuation and marking-to-market
- To outline best practices that market participants should develop in order to measure, track and adequately capitalize for the "market risks" associated with their portfolios.

Credit Risk Objectives

- To identify, standardize and require the tracking of key metrics which measure credit risk
- To increase risk transparency to improve stakeholder understanding of credit risk carried by market participants
- To outline credit risk "best practices" that market participants should develop in order

to reduce credit losses, make better reserve and capital allocation decisions, and improve earnings predictability.

Capital Adequacy Objectives

- Establish connection between risk inherent in business activities and capital necessary to withstand a downside event
- Leverage and establish linkage with currently used measures of risk such as value-at-risk, credit value-at-risk, credit exposure, reserves, etc.
- Capital required should be a function of risk and actual or target credit rating credit quality
- While a very useful measure for internal management purposes, initial focus should be on providing meaningful risk quantification to external parties, e.g., investment community, regulators, rating agencies
- While all risks should be considered, initial focus should be on market and credit risk and its impact on capital needs

Compliance Objectives

Assuming that an effective set of Risk Management Standards are developed, a method for assuring compliance with the standards becomes essential to re-gain the confidence of investors, analysts, rating agencies, regulators and legislators.

A key issue that must be considered is the degree of formality associated with the compliance process – the compliance tolerance. The Task Force reviewed the key

POWER MARKET RISK

dynamics surrounding what should be considered a continuum of compliance options. The options range from least formal to most formal.

The least formal is the voluntary, "take my word," option where participants formally declare their intent to comply with the standards in public forums and confirm their compliance by statements in quarterly and annual disclosures. This option is the easiest to implement and is the safest from a management viewpoint since it requires limited additional disclosure. However, pursuing this option, says the Task Force, will invite skepticism from investors, analysts, and others, and may be seen as "too soft" by regulators and legislators given the existing political environment.

Voluntary disclosure is the middle option. Under this option, standards-related measures are added to quarterly and annual disclosures. In addition, standards-related performance is discussed on analyst and rating agency conference calls and at meetings. Finally, compliance is verified by internal audit. This option, says NEMA, represents a "compromise" level of compliance. It would likely require changes to participant's risk management capabilities and metrics. Lastly, capability enhancements would likely require investments.

The most formal option is audited compliance. Under this option, standards are added to annual independent audit templates, and an independent auditor attests to the participant's compliance with standards. This is the most rigorous of the compliance options and would likely require changes to participant's risk management capabilities and metrics. Moreover, capability enhancements would likely require investments for companies taking this approach. One of the benefits of this option is that investors, analysts, ratings agencies and other may view independent verification as the most credible compliance measures. Further, this option may be the best fit considering current political dynamics.

Governance Objectives

- Articulate a code of conduct which addresses unacceptable trading and accounting actions such as those recently revealed (wash trades, market manipulation, etc.)
- Clearly define and document corporate risk policy
- Define and implement a risk governance framework which establishes appropriate levels of oversight and checks-and-balances, including: Board of Directors, CEO, Executive Committee, Risk Management Committee, and CRO as well as trading functions and controls for front office, middle office, and back office.
- Demonstrate a company has oversight on trading strategies which would prevent "wash trades" and other questionable actions
- Establish trader compensation plans that exclude incentives for questionable actions
- Fully disclose governance measures to market stakeholders

Why are these standards necessary? Says Goodman: "During the beginning of any restructuring, you are going to have a weeding out of the good, the better, and the best. The unexpected shock was that because electricity isn't storable, because it's the most volatile commodity in the marketplace today, and because there were no master netting agreements in place, the law didn't anticipate an

Enron-style bankruptcy. What has also come to light is how aggressively lawyers and accountants have been interpreting existing laws and how aggressively Wall Street has been setting unrealistically high expectations for future growth rates."

"In my opinion, corporate leadership must start under promising and over performing to regain the credibility that investors, consumers, and regulators must have to rebuild our industry. I think there are ways of stating information in a plain, ordinary way so that an average investor can truly understand what the financial condition of a company is. I don't think it's hard to do that. We are close to having guidelines for credit and risk valuation, management, and financial accountability," Goodman says.

The Committee of CROs

Like NEM, Chief Risk Officers are concerned about best practices and standardization. In order to work on common standards, a group of merchant energy companies formed the Committee of CROs. The group grew from a short list of charter companies -- American Electric Power, Constellation Energy Group, Duke Energy, Tractebel North American, Inc., Mirant, and TXU – to include 31 energy companies.

"Due to recent market events and the increased scrutiny being placed on companies involved in energy trading and marketing, it is important for those of us actively involved in the industry to take constructive steps to define risk management practices and communicate these standards to our stakeholders," commented Mayo A. Shattuck, III, president and CEO of Constellation when the Committee was launched in May 2002.

There are four areas of focus for the Committee, says

POWER MARKET RISK

G. Patrich Simpkins, executive vice president and CRO of TXU. "They are: To define best practices, to define consistent application, to define common measures, and to enhance transparency relative to disclosures, credit, organizational independence, risk evaluation, and metrics. That's what we're tackling." Simpkins notes.

"TXU has representation on the credit and disclosure committees and other subcommittees. We are actively involved, as are the other participants," he comments.

The Committee of CROs is "an interesting group," says Scott Smith, CRO of AEP. "You have small, medium and large players. It isn't AEP, and Duke, and Mirant running this. We all face the same issues, like credit."

Smith is the co-chair of the valuation and market risk subcommittee, which is trying to develop a best practice document similar to the Group of Thirty report. "We need that," he comments. And, as you'll see, the group has done just that. The group is trying to standardize valuation approaches so it's easier to compare one company's reporting with another's.

In November 2002, the Committee released its recommendations on governance, valuation and risk metrics, credit risk management, and disclosure. The main recommendations for merchant energy companies are:

Governance

- Minimize operational risks by strict segregation of responsibilities for trading, valuation and accounting
- Ensure the Chief Risk Officer is independent of the trading operation
- Establish a company-wide framework with specific risk tolerances for trading energy and re-

lated derivatives

Valuation and Risk Metrics

- Systematically analyze the value and risk of merchant energy activities
- Develop performance and risk metrics for internal management and external disclosure
- ·Evaluate the effects of sudden and extreme events on the company's overall trading portfolio

Credit Risk Management

- Adopt and implement a clearing platform and multilateral netting agreements
- Measure the risk of possible defaults by trading partners and ratings changes by credit rating agencies
- ·Establish credit limits based on a quantitative and qualitative analysis of a company's overall portfolio, exposure to trading partners and the cost of credit

Disclosure

- Adhere to the Committee's principles of comparability, consistency, relevancy, standardization and transparency
- Summarize important information in tables that reflect each company's merchant energy business activities and are easy to compare among companies
- Separate proprietary trading activities

POWER MARKET RISK

from other merchant energy activities

What's ahead? The Committee is assessing how it "might provide guidance on creating more credible and verifiable forms of market price indices," the group says.

In addition, the Committee is "working with other advocacy groups," points out Simpkins. "We want to make sure that we're in alignment and that they're in alignment with us. We also want to get together with other advocacy groups that have the political power to drive some of these changes through the industry. It's something that should transcend more than just our industry."

The efforts of both NEM and the Committee of CROs are welcome. But the industry doesn't need two sets of standards. For the industry to move forward, the two groups should collaborate to create one standard for the power markets. When that happens, we truly will have a Group of Thirty report done by the energy industry.

Chapter 15:
Rolling The Crystal Ball: Some Predictions

So, where is the utility industry headed? And what role does risk management have to play in its future success? We think we've shown you what the problems *are*, and how risk management can help alleviate or solve them. But since the industry is in a state of change, it's worth speculating a little on how the next few years may shake out. All of these possible future developments will require study and action by risk managers. Now is a good time to start thinking about them. You may agree or disagree with some or all of the following, but to neglect to assess them would be to increase your future risks.

Trading Will Rebound

Energy trading, and electricity trading in particular, will recover some momentum in the next three to four years. At the time of writing, we've seen a terrible bloodbath in trading rooms, and companies have pulled back in their activities. Longer term, trading will regain its respectability – helped in no small measure by responsible practices and intelligent risk management. Electricity can't effectively be stored, it has to flow to where it's going to be used.

Demographics Favor Electricity

US population growth is a constant, both through domestic population growth and immigration. Cities continue to sprawl, and suburbs grow. Households will require more power, even though energy efficiency will dull the growth somewhat.

Deregulation is Here To Stay

You can't put the genie back in the bottle. It may be that we will see more structure to deregulation efforts in the future, and some of the Ohio and California mistakes will be avoided, with the wisdom of hindsight. But the road to deregulation started with PURPA back in 1976, opening the door to cogenerators. It's a train that probably can't – or shouldn't – be stopped.

Energy Will Become More Expensive

We can kiss off nuclear power in the longer term, through attrition, as older plants begin to close down. Although the Bush Administration's nascent energy policy calls for a resumption of building nuclear power plants, it's hard to imagine how this will happen, without government indemnification of the costs on the fuel management and waste management ends of the nuclear cycle. Although nuclear proponents cite the example of France as a country that has 'succeeded' with nuclear power, it's worth remembering that the French nuclear system survives behind a protectionist barrier.

POWER MARKET RISK

Hydro power is under pressure, and no one is likely to take on the risk of building new dams. In fact, there's strong environmental pressure to remove some older structures.

Thus gas-fired, or (less likely) efficient coal-fired generation will assume the load. There are no real alternatives. We can't count on wind or solar power in the next ten years, nor geothermal, nor tidal or any of the other 'sounds good' quasi-'green' technologies. Among them, solar power is the best bet – developments in the field of photonics technology are increasing the efficiency of solar collectors by leaps and bounds. There are still plenty of bugs to be engineered out of wind power, though the technology has improved markedly in the past five years.

The situation for oil exploration and development of new fields is not very promising – and when coupled with volatile mid-East politics – does not offer much hope for lower hydrocarbon prices in future.

Knowledge Management Will Redefine RM

Enterprises know so much about what's going on, but realize so little, because they are literally drowning in information. KM is going to change the culture over the next ten years, both for marketers and for risk managers.

New Players Will Appear

There is no reason why oil companies should not become a force in electricity. They are major players in oil and natural gas supply, and in coal in some cases. They know how to run process plants, and operating a simple piece of hardware like a power generator is not beyond their capabilities (many, after all, are significant co-generators). Many are involved in the retail gasoline business, with

POWER MARKET RISK

credit cards issued and payment systems in place. Initially, their strategy may be to seek 'low fruit' like industrial customers, or large energy-consuming facilities like shopping malls. Longer term, you might expect to see them compete for the domestic base, too.

Billing & Metering Has To Become Smarter

The technology is here. There is immense competitive advantage to be gained by deploying ways of assessing consumer's bills on an hourly basis. And there's a fundamentally good reason for implementing it. In the words of one expert who has spent time on the issue: "The business now is spot price risk management. That's the essence of why you have trading. It is in the best interest of everyone in this industry to have the demand side be more intelligent and educated. Companies should be strong supporters of things like metering technology. If you can get consumers to have their meters read on an hourly basis and be active participants in the spot market, that's going to benefit everyone."

"Consumers are simply providers of megawatts, just like generators. Consumers are like a base load provider in that they provide a base load of consumption. Consumers could respond at the margin to prices, but they have no incentive to do that because of regulatory barriers at the state level. Consumers are charged the same price for every megawatt they consume. Imagine if you paid the producer of electricity the same price for every megawatt he supplied, whether it was in the peak period or the off period! Well, you don't do that on the generation side. But on the load side, that's what you do. The big reason you do that is because meters get read only at the start of the month and the end of the month and record the total consumption for the month."

"The attitude in the power markets is that we'd rather have a lot of dumb demand, that doesn't respond to the hourly price because that's going to help us make a lot of money in the market. But power marketers need to be major supporters of demand side participation and symmetric treatment of load and generation. That's where the long-term benefit of the market lies as well as the chance to make some money. They are being short sighted by not recognizing it."

"Some local power companies are interested in installing online electronic metering technology that could read meters on an hourly, or half-hourly, basis. This would need to be done on a regional basis. A lot of the power marketers are fighting this. But when you get the demand side involved, there's money to be made as a power marketer. The power marketers can offer customers risk management services. If a meter can be read on an hourly basis, power marketers can offer customers 30 times 24 different prices for the different hours in the month. That means lots more dimensions where competition can take place. And more opportunity for energy management."

"If we are going to have supply to dumb demand, it's hard to argue that markets can do that better than regulation. A market works very well when suppliers and consumers respond to the prices they can see."

Resources and References

The following list of resources is a selected list of materials available on risk management for the power markets. It is presented for informational purposes only and does not constitute a recommendation or endorsement.

Reports, White Papers, Books & Magazine Articles

Federal Energy Regulatory Commission (FERC). *Initial Report On Company-Specific Separate Proceedings And Generic Reevaluations; Published Natural Gas Price Data; And Enron Trading Strategies. Fact-Finding Investigation Of Potential Manipulation Of Electric And Natural Gas Prices*; Docket No. PA02-2-000. (August 2002), 112 pp. Federal Energy Regulatory Commission (FERC), 888 First Street, N.E., Washington, DC 20426. Online at: http://www.ferc.gov/Electric/bulkpower/PA02-2/Initial-Report-PA02-2-000.pdf

Financial Accounting Standards Board Emerging Issues Task Force. Accounting for Contracts Involved in Energy Trading and Risk Management Activities, Issue No. 98-10. July 1999.

Financial Accounting Standards Board Emerging Issues Task Force. *Accounting for Weather Derivatives, Issue No. 99-2.* July 1999.

Financial Accounting Standards Board. *Statement of Financial Accounting Standards No. 133.* Norwalk: June 1998.

Financial Accounting Standards Board. *Statement of Financial Accounting Standards No. 137.* Norwalk: June 1999.

Global Derivatives Study Group, The Group of Thirty, *Derivatives: Practices and Principles*, Washington DC, July 1993. The Group of Thirty can be contacted at 1990 M. Street, NW, Washington DC 20036. Tel: 202/331-2472. Fax: 202/785-9423. Copies of the Derivatives report may be purchased through the website: The website is: http://www.group30.org/

Kramer, Andrea S. and Harris, Alton B. "Derivatives and Legal Risks: Practical Protective Steps," *The Review of Banking & Financial Services*. Vol. 11, No. 22 December 17, 1995.

Kramer, Andrea S. *Financial Products: Taxation, Regulation and Design*, 3rd. Edition, New York: Panel Publishers. 2000.

Kramer, Andrea S. Items to Consider for Trading and Derivatives Policies, Guidelines, Controls, and Internal Procedures. 2002.

Kramer, Andrea S. and Pantano, Paul J. Jr. "Managing

Hidden Legal Risks," *Hart Energy Markets.* Vol. 4, No. 11 November 1999.

Lese, Andrew and Hakanson, Roger. "Managing Not To Worry." *Energy & Power Risk Management,* May 1999.

Senate Committee on Governmental Affairs. *Committee Staff Investigation of the Federal Energy Regulatory Commission's Oversight of Enron Corp.* November 12, 2002, 51pp. Governmental Affairs Committee, US Senate, 340 Dirksen Senate Office Building Washington, DC 20510. Online at: http://www.senate.gov/~gov_affairs/111202fercmemo.pdf

United States General Accounting Office Financial Derivatives: Actions Needed to Protect the Financial System, Washington DC, May 1994.

Williams, Mark. "Knowing the Score." *Energy & Power Risk Management,* May 1999.

Education
Andrea S. Kramer, a partner with McDermott, Will & Emery, conducts risk management training seminars. In addition, you can obtain copies of her guide, "Items to Consider for Trading and Derivatives Policies, Guidelines, Controls and Internal Procedures," by emailing her at akramer@mwe.com.
For further information, contact:
Andrea S. Kramer
McDermott, Will & Emery
227 West Monroe St.,
Chicago IL 60606
Tel: 312/984-6480

Government Agencies

The Commodity Futures Trading Commission
Three Lafayette Centre
1155 21st St., NW
Washington DC 20581
Tel: 202/418-5000
Fax: 202/418-5521
Internet: www.cftc.gov

Futures Exchanges

Chicago Mercantile Exchange
30 South Wacker Drive
Chicago IL 60606
Tel: 312/930-1000
Internet: www.cme.com

New York Mercantile Exchange
World Financial Center
One North End Avenue
New York NY 10282
Tel: 212/299-2000
Internet: www.nymex.com
The NYMEX offers natural gas, electricity, coal, crude oil, propane, gasoline and heating oil futures and options.

Associations and Organizations

Committee of Chief Risk Officers
E-mail: info@ccro.org
Website: www.ccro.org

Edison Electric Institute
701 Pennsylvania Avenue, NW

Washington DC 20004
Tel: 202/508-5000
Internet: www.eei.org

Financial Accounting Standards Board
401 Merritt 7,
PO Box 5116
Norwalk CT 06856-5116
Tel: 203/847-0700
Fax: 203/849-9714
Internet: www.fasb.org
Copies of any of the FASB statements such as Statement No.133 can be ordered through the organization.

National Energy Marketers Association,
3333 K Street, NW
Suite 425
Washington, DC 20007
Tel: 202/ 333-3288
Website: www.energymarketers.com

North American Energy Standards Board, Inc.
1100 Louisiana
Suite 3625
Houston TX 77002
Tel: 713/356-0060
Fax: 713/356-0067
E-mail: naesb@aol.com
Internet: www.gisb.org

International Swaps & Derivatives Association
360 Madison Avenue
16th Floor
New York NY 10017
Tel: 212/901-6000

POWER MARKET RISK

Fax: 212/901-6001
Internet: www.isda.org
Copies of all ISDA documents such as the master agreements may be purchased from the association. The website has a complete list of documents, prices and ordering information.

Weather Risk Management Association
1156 15th Street NW, Suite 900
Washington DC 20005
Tel: 202/289-3800
Fax: 202/223-9741
E-mail: wrma@kellencompany.com
Internet: www.wrma.org

About the Authors

Shirley S. Savage is President of The Thinking Companies, Inc. Prior to starting The Thinking Companies, Inc., she was an energy journalist for 25 years, well known for her authoritative coverage of oil and coal markets for *Platt's Oilgram Price Report*, *Coal Week* and *Coal Week International*, published by The McGraw-Hill Companies. She has also covered banking and finance for *Global Finance* magazine. A graduate of the University of Illinois, Champaign-Urbana, Shirley is a director of the Professional Consultants of Maine. She authored *Power Market Risk Management* for *Financial Times Energy,* and writes the newsletter of the Weather Risk Management Association.

Peter R. Savage ('The Ideas Guy') is a principal of The Thinking Companies, Inc. In his 30 years as a journalist for McGraw-Hill, John Wiley & Sons and others, Peter is recognized for his ability to report and write about the chemical industry, energy, technology, banking, and finance for publications like *Chemical Week*, *Business Week, IEEE Spectrum* and the family of Technical Insights newsletters. As a consultant he worked for Chem Systems, among others. Peter is a graduate of University College, London. He is a member of the American Chemical Society, the American Association for the Advancement of Science, and Professional Consultants of Maine. He is currently finishing a book on business ethics and governance.

The Thinking Companies was established to provide clients with usable knowledge about the intellectual and technological challenges of the 21st century. It specializes in such subjects as alternative energy, business strategy, and monitoring cutting edge developments in the fields of nanotechnology and electronics.